"Our lives get more busy yet more empty[...] describes what you feel and why you feel like that, and walks with you to a better way. And, somehow, he does it in a way that makes you feel heard, even befriended. Within two pages you will be drawn in by Steve's honesty and how he seems to speak to *you*. Then you read the entire book—hope rising with each chapter. Since one chapter will be uniquely yours, you will double back, re-read that chapter, and act on that hope."

ED WELCH, *Counselor and faculty member at the Christian Counseling & Educational Foundation (CCEF)*

"Steve grabs your attention from the very first sentence. He sheds unique insight into idolatry through vivid imagery and solid biblical instruction. He powerfully points you to the only One who can and will quench your thirst. I will be sharing this book with those I counsel— both professing Christians and those who profess no faith at all."

TIMOTHY LANE, *President of the Institute for Pastoral Care and co-author of "How People Change"*

"The idea that we are constantly sipping saltwater is an extremely helpful image which is then carefully applied to our battle with sin. This book is beautifully honest, packed with stories, and ultimately full of hope in Christ."

JONTY ALLCOCK, *Lead Pastor, The Globe Church, London, and author of "Lost," "Fearless" and "Hero"*

"In *Sipping Saltwater*, Steve Hoppe draws on his vast experience as a pastor and counselor. He writes not as an aloof professional, but rather, as a fellow traveler—broken, flawed, and in search of full redemption. With clarity and directness, he weaves together the timeless truths of Scripture, real-life stories of people in the pews, and his own journey of moving from brokenness to wholeness."

MINDY MEIER, *Author, speaker, and Associate Director of Greek InterVarsity Christian Fellowship*

"Steve Hoppe uses vivid imagery and powerful stories to explain a problem plaguing us all—idolatry. But he doesn't stop there. He gets practical by digging into dozens of everyday idols and showing how Christ is better than them all."

GABE LYONS, *President of Q Ideas and author of "Good Faith"*

"This book has been so good for my foolish, thirsty heart, which so easily defaults to drinking deadly 'saltwater.' With great warmth, honesty, and insight, Steve exposes and redirects our hearts to the Lord Jesus, the only One who can and does quench our thirst and bring joy to our hearts."

ANDREA TREVENNA, *Associate for Women's Ministry, St Nicholas Church, Sevenoaks, UK*

"*Sipping Saltwater* is an invitation to find lasting satisfaction for our deepest longings. Steve offers biblical and relevant ways to think differently about work, sex, money, comfort, control, and much more. Compelling, practical, and transparent. I could not put this book down!"

PETER GREER, *President and CEO of HOPE International, and co-author of "Mission Drift"*

"Surrounded by saltwater inside the gut of a fish, the prophet Jonah said that when we cling to worthless idols, we forfeit the grace that could be ours. *Sipping Saltwater* is a thoughtful, helpful field guide on the idols Jonah grieved for, and to which we, too, are all susceptible. I highly recommend this book."

SCOTT SAULS, *Senior Pastor of Christ Presbyterian Church in Nashville, Tennessee, and author of "Befriend" and "From Weakness to Strength"*

"With a pastor's heart, a counselor's eye, and a historian's love of story, Steve draws from each to produce a helpful book on the idols of the heart. Steve unpacks the dynamics around why we return to destructive choices, even when we know they are destroying us. With insight that comes from years of walking alongside others, Steve sees into the human heart and provides hope for healing its brokenness. This book is real, a bit gritty, and immensely helpful!"

NIKKI TOYAMA-SZETO, *Executive Director, Evangelicals for Social Action (ESA)*

"How often have we all thought, 'Why do I keep doing the same unwise things over and over again?' In *Sipping Saltwater* Steve pulls back the curtain to help us understand what our unhealthy motives are and how the gospel can bring hope, clarity, and change to the darkest areas of our lives."

JACKSON CRUM, *Lead Pastor, Park Community Church, Chicago*

SIPPING
SALTWATER

STEVE HOPPE

thegoodbook
COMPANY

To Dad. I'll see you soon.

Sipping Saltwater *How to Find Lasting Satisfaction in a World of Thirst*
© Steve Hoppe/The Good Book Company, 2017. Reprinted 2018.

Published by
The Good Book Company
Tel (UK): 0333 123 0880
International: +44 (0) 208 942 0880
Email: info@thegoodbook.co.uk

Websites:
North America: www.thegoodbook.com
UK: www.thegoodbook.co.uk
Australia: www.thegoodbook.com.au
New Zealand: www.thegoodbook.co.nz

This book includes many illustrations. Please note that some of the names
and identifying details have been changed to preserve anonymity.

Unless indicated, all Scripture references are taken from the HOLY BIBLE,
NEW INTERNATIONAL VERSION. Copyright © 2011 Biblica, Inc.™ Used
by permission.

Cover design by ninefootone creative

ISBN: 9781784981822 | Printed in the UK

CONTENTS

THIRST

"Water, water, every where,
Nor any drop to drink."

Samuel Taylor Coleridge, *The Rime of the Ancient Mariner*

"Prepare to crash."

These were the last words spoken on the Green Hornet. In the spring of 1943, the American World War II combat plane and its eleven crewmen set off on a search-and-rescue mission over the Pacific Ocean. Roughly 200 miles into the trip, the plane lost its two left engines, spiraled toward the sea, and exploded upon impact.

On the Green Hornet was Louie Zamperini—a national celebrity at the time. Louie had finished eighth in the 5,000-meter run at the 1936 Berlin Olympics and was predicted to run the first sub-four-minute mile. The good news? Louie somehow survived the crash unscathed. The bad news? He was stranded in the middle of the largest ocean in the world. And nobody knew he was there.

Louie faced brutal challenges as he drifted for 47 days on the Pacific. His skin burned with sun blisters and salt sores. His swollen lips pressed forcefully into his nose and chin. Without food, he lost almost two pounds a day. To top it off, he had two enemies after him. The first came from below—a posse of twelve-foot sharks mockingly rubbing their backs against his flimsy inflatable raft. The second came from above—the Japanese. After weeks of aimlessly drifting, Louie was spotted by one of their planes. They shot up his raft. Somehow, they missed Louie.

Yet, with these and other challenges threatening Louie's life, perhaps the greatest threat to his survival came from within.

Thirst.

Thirst? How could this be? All he could see in every direction was water. Cool, crisp, clear water. It looked like drinking water, felt like drinking water, and even sounded like drinking water. How could thirst be an issue?

Louie was surrounded by 64 million square miles of *saltwater*. And he couldn't take a sip.

What would have happened if Louie drank the surrounding sea? First, the saltwater would have dried out his insides and left him thirstier than before. Second, he would have experienced the worst hangover of his life. He would have suffered explosive diarrhea, a pounding headache, muscle cramps, dizziness, a dry mouth, vomiting, increased blood pressure, a rapid heart rate, kidney failure, hallucinations, and seizures. If he kept drinking, he would have fallen into a coma, experienced massive organ failure, and sustained irreparable brain damage. Eventually, drinking saltwater would have killed him.

Louie resisted the urge to sip from the Pacific. And he survived. Not without a struggle. But he survived.

Why do I start with this story?

Because unlike Louie, *we drink saltwater*. Some people gulp it down. Most of us take tiny sips without realizing it.

And that's what this book is about...

1. OUR NAGGING THIRST

My father died while I was writing this book.

As I reflect on his life of 67 years, one thing stands out. It isn't his intelligence, which was exceptional. It isn't his witty sense of humor, which charmed people wherever he went. It isn't his long list of professional accomplishments, which his humility prevented him from ever revealing. It isn't his good looks, charisma, or attractive ability to self-deprecate. While these were surely defining characteristics of my father, one thing stands out above the rest.

My father was an alcoholic.

Unfortunately, my memories of my dad are dominated by an array of events, experiences, stories, situations, sights, smells, and sounds directly linked with his 40-year drinking problem. I remember him attempting to coach my basketball team but being too drunk to dribble the ball. I remember him trying to pitch at Little League batting practice but being too drunk to throw a strike. I remember him breaking his leg after a drunken fall outside his Chicago law office. I remember the pungent smell of beer and Listerine that told me he was home from work. I remember the subtle slur in his voice that signaled yet another night of fighting between him and my mom. I remember crying in my bedroom while she desperately begged him to get help. I remember him insisting that he didn't need it. I remember his frequent yet empty promises to change. I remember feeling constantly confused, disappointed, sad, and embarrassed to be the son of an alcoholic.

I remember so much. A little good. And a whole lot of bad.

Growing up, it made no sense to me why my father drank so much. He was a handsome and brilliant Ivy League graduate working as an attorney for one of the most prestigious law firms in Chicago. He had a devoted wife and three healthy children who he loved and who loved him greatly. He lived in a beautiful suburban home and had more than enough money. Above all, he was a really nice guy. Everybody liked him. Everybody. However, after every day of work he still drank beer after beer until he was stone-cold drunk. Every. Single. Day.

Eventually he lost everything. He lost his dream job and a series of successive jobs that gradually diminished in prestige and pay. He lost his wife, who divorced him after eighteen years of marriage. He lost his children and was forced to accept the role of a weekend-only dad. He lost his quaint suburban home, eventually landing in a dingy one-bedroom apartment in the low-income section of a neighboring town. He lost tens of thousands of dollars. He lost countless relationships. He lost his dignity. He lost his reputation. He lost everything.

And yet he continued to drink.

Why?

A Thirst for Paradise

Why did my father drink so much? Why did he consciously choose to slam beer after beer, knowing the terrible consequences of each and every sip? Why did he willingly keep consuming a substance that was ruining his life? Why would my dad choose beer over everything else of value to him?

The knee-jerk answer is simple—addiction. My father was addicted to alcohol. He started drinking in college as a stress-release valve, continued drinking to cope with the challenges of marriage and fatherhood, and eventually became hooked. The addiction took over his mind, body, and soul. It ruled him. And he let it rule him.

But this explanation isn't good enough. Why not? Simply labeling my father an addict doesn't get at the root of his problem. It barely scratches the surface. There's a deeper, more profound reason why he chose to drink in the first place and continued to do so even after he lost everything. It starts with one word.

Thirst.

My father was thirsty. I'm not talking about a physical thirst for beer. This thirst wasn't physical. It was spiritual. Although he didn't realize it, my father was thirsty for something more than beer could offer. More than this *world* could offer. Something more satisfying. Something more powerful. Something more gratifying, refreshing, and rewarding. Something that could fill the nagging void in his heart. Something that could bring peace to his unsettled soul. Something that could remove his existential emptiness. Something transcendent.

Something heavenly.

My father had a thirst for paradise. He tried to quench it with beer, but it couldn't do the trick.

The Bible talks about this thirst for paradise in the book of Ecclesiastes. There, the author says that God has "set eternity in the human heart" (Ecclesiastes 3 v 11). In other words, God has created us—all of us—with a restless yearning for a never-ending, perfect world. A world of boundless love, comfort, and beauty. A world in which we can never smile enough, laugh enough, or play enough. A world in which our bodies remain strong, our minds remain sharp, and our hearts remain pure. A world without fighting, fearing, or failing. A world without sickness. A world without wounds. A world where *nothing* hurts. A world of bottomless pleasure and infinite joy.

A world we can't get by cracking open a beer.

We're born thirsty for a world beyond this one. We're thirsty for paradise. My dad was. We all are.

But this presents a problem.

Our world *isn't* paradise. Our jobs are stressful, taxing, and unfulfilling. Our relationships are quarrelsome. We get cancer. We break bones, throw up, and get hemorrhoids. We feel nervous, afraid, angry, and upset. The Holocaust happens. 9/11 happens. Poverty, genocide, and starvation happen. Terrorists set off bombs. Our cars hit potholes. Books are ridiculously difficult to write. We go years without speaking to relatives. Divorce splits families. Hurricanes, tsunamis, and earthquakes destroy the planet. Love fades. World peace is a clichéd impossibility. We get wrinkles, zits, sunspots, and bald spots. We rarely smile. We rarely laugh. We rarely let loose and play. Our minds fail us. Our hearts ache. We constantly itch for more.

Eventually we die.

The world as we know it is anything but paradise.

Why? Why is paradise nowhere to be found?

Paradise Lost

The answer goes back to first book of the Bible: the book of Genesis. In Genesis chapter 2, we're introduced to the original paradise—the Garden of Eden. We're also introduced to the dynamic naked duo of Adam and Eve—the first human residents of this paradise.

In the garden, Adam and Eve have a unique privilege. They're allowed to live with God. They can speak directly to him, listen to his audible voice, and experience every ounce of pleasure he provides. They're roommates with God. Their home is heaven on earth. Forever.

There's just one rule. A simple dietary restriction. God tells them they can't eat from one tree—the tree of the knowledge of good and evil. Why not? A bite of its fruit would give them a heightened level of wisdom that would lead to independence from God instead of dependence on him. If Adam and Eve eat from this tree, God promises that their eternal life in paradise will be stripped. They're promised death.

Next, the devil—disguised as a serpent—enters the scene and deceives Eve.

> You will not certainly die ... For God knows that when
> you eat from it your eyes will be opened, and you will be
> like God, knowing good and evil. (Genesis 3 v 4-5)

The serpent calls God a liar. He tells Eve she won't die if she eats the forbidden fruit. In fact, he promises she'll be God-like if she takes a bite. And Eve takes the bait. She bites into the fruit and her husband follows her lead.

God's response? He punishes them. He tells Eve that childbirth will be agonizing and marriage will be a power struggle. He then tells Adam that his job as a farmer will be exhausting. The ground will be cursed, his body will be inadequate, and he'll work until the day he dies, at which point he'll return to the cursed ground from which he came (Genesis 3 v 16-19).

But worst of all, they're expelled from paradise.

After Adam and Eve eat the forbidden fruit, God casts them out of Eden. Never to return. Never to live in the home God originally intended for them. Never to experience the joy, beauty, delight, and satisfaction he meant for them. They're banished from paradise, sentenced to die apart from God.

And so are we. We've also been banished from paradise. You have. I have. We all have.

Same Team

Why have we been banished from paradise?

We're on the same team as Adam and Eve. We're just as greedy. Just as self-centered. Just as rebellious. Just as sinful. In fact, we've inherited their sinful nature. We're ruled by the passions of our egocentric hearts. We follow our flawed wisdom. We do things we shouldn't and don't do things we should. We belittle our spouses, disrespect our parents, and ignore our children. We cheat on our taxes, tithes, and time cards. We're passive aggressive, profane, and proud. We forget to give thanks, refuse to sacrifice, and stink at love. We're on Adam and Eve's team of rebels against God.

So we face the same consequence as them. We've been expelled from God's presence—cast out of the metaphorical garden. Instead of coexisting with him face to face in eternal euphoria, we're separated from him in this world—a world filled with suffering and turmoil.

Paradise is nowhere to be found.

Meltdown in Michigan

I became painfully aware that life was *anything* but paradise during my freshman year at the University of Michigan.

To the outside eye, my life was incredible. I was at my dream school in a top engineering program. I lived on a lively co-ed floor with a cohort of down-to-earth, light-hearted hallmates. I had a lovely girlfriend at a nearby college who I saw every other weekend. I was in a top-notch fraternity. My school won the national championship in both football and hockey that year. I *should* have been happy.

Instead, I had a nervous breakdown.

A week after my college arrival, I became consumed with inexplicable anxiety. From the second I woke up until the moment I went to bed, I felt as if I had nine cups of coffee in my system. My thoughts raced. My heart pounded. Sleep was rare. Panic attacks were routine. I was paranoid—obsessively questioning my girlfriend's faithfulness for no reason. On multiple occasions I had to leave group study sessions because I was nervously dripping with sweat. Depression eventually set in. I spent many nights roaming the campus weeping. I felt alone in my dysfunctional head.

I decided to reach out for help. Over Thanksgiving break I met with a psychologist. She listened well and taught me some helpful breathing exercises. But the anxiety didn't subside. Over Christmas break I saw a psychiatrist. She put me on a strong dose of antidepressants and asked a lot about my sex life. Neither the drugs nor the sex talk helped.

I returned to school for my second semester and things got worse. Suddenly the classroom became nerve-wracking. I became anxious about being anxious, which only made me more anxious. I couldn't eat or sleep. I felt trapped. I wanted to escape.

To where?

I had no idea. A place without anxiety? A place where I didn't feel crippled and crazy on the inside? A place where I didn't appear distant and awkward on the outside? Where I was mentally stable? Where there were no more heart palpitations, stress headaches, or excessive sweating episodes? Where people accepted me? Where nervousness, crying, and paranoia were no more? A world without suffering?

Although I wouldn't have said so, I was thirsty for paradise.

And God was offering it. He was offering a beverage that *would* have quenched my thirst for paradise lost. One that would have quenched my dad's thirst. One that will quench yours. One that satisfies not just your body, but your soul. One more pure, precious, potent, and pleasing than anything this world can provide. One that God offers me every day. One that he's offering you. One offered to anybody who'll drink it. *Anybody*.

But I foolishly turned down the offer. I looked elsewhere to satisfy my thirst. I sipped a different drink.

You might be sipping it too.

What drink did I sip? Read on and find out...

2. OUR DRINK OF CHOICE

In the drink.

It was a popular expression describing World War II plane-crash survivors stranded in the ocean. When Louie Zamperini landed in the middle of the Pacific, he was "in the drink."

Though the term was catchy and poetic, there was a problem with it. It wasn't true. Louie wasn't in the drink. He knew drinking the surrounding sea would have been catastrophic. It would not have quenched his thirst but left him thirstier. It would not have eased his discomfort but exacerbated it. It would not have prolonged his life but ended it.

Louie knew he wasn't really in the drink.

If only we were so wise.

Promising Paradise

In our nagging state of thirst for paradise lost, what do we drink? *Saltwater.* We consume things that look and feel and sound like they can quench our thirst. They promise unmatched pleasure. They promote limitless comfort, joy, strength, peace, and excitement. They vow to remove our fears, tears, worries, guilt, and shame. They pledge to fill the voids in our hearts and soothe our aching souls. They promise paradise.

But they can't deliver. We drink them, but our thirst remains unquenched. In fact, we're left thirstier. And we experience devastating hangovers—negative spiritual, emotional, physical, and relational consequences—as a result.

No, this saltwater doesn't come from the ocean. It comes in a variety of forms from the world around us and our hearts within. It comes in the form of money, sex, control, or comfort. It comes in the form of busyness, people, food, or works. It can come in the form of *anything*. For my father, it came in the form of booze.

Even though we're thirsty for paradise lost, we drink saltwater instead—in a million different forms.

How Many A's Does It Take?

Back to the nervous breakdown I experienced during my freshman year of college. How did I respond?

I drank saltwater. What form? Academics. In an effort to regain control over my life, I poured everything I had into school. I studied when I woke up. I studied between classes. I studied during meals. I studied on Friday nights while my fraternity brothers hit the bars. I studied on Saturday afternoons while my roommates threw Frisbees, watched football, and played video games. I skipped church on Sundays to study. I spent holidays studying. I was *always* studying.

In December I got my first semester report card. Four A's and one A-.

I felt better. My thirst was quenched.

For 15 minutes.

After the rush wore off, I was thirsty again. Actually, thirstier. I wanted even *better* grades. So I worked even harder. I started copying down entire textbook chapters to absorb the material more thoroughly. I did problem sets five times to make sure I wouldn't be fooled come test time. I memorized class notes word for word. I attended every office hour available. Eventually I was spending 16-18 hours a day working on academics.

In May I got my second semester report card. Another four A's and one A-. This time, there was no rush. In fact, I felt disappointed.

From that point on, only straight A's would do.

I achieved the feat in the first semester of my sophomore year. And again second semester. By my junior year, I became numb to the high of an A and needed something more. I found it—the almost-impossible-to-achieve A+. Once I got a few of these, I had a new goal—straight A+'s. *That* would satisfy me. *That* would quench my thirst. Right? I never found out. I peaked at four A+'s and one A during my senior year.

One *lousy* A.

My Hangover

After drinking gallons of saltwater that freshman year, I suffered two painful hangover symptoms. First, my relationships deteriorated. My fraternity brothers revoked my membership because I was unwilling to hang out at the house. My roommates quit inviting me to parties, assuming I'd be studying anyways. My girlfriend asked for space, annoyed at my new obsession with school. The more I studied, the more unlikable I became. And people rightly pushed me away.

My second hangover symptom was a *new* form of anxiety—the fear of failure. When I received an assignment back with a B or (gasp!) a C on it, my anxiety shot through the roof. My only coping mechanism was to hit the books harder, sleep less, and study more. By the time final exams came, I could usually teach my classes better than my professors. Not because I was smart. I was *obsessed.* I was gulping down the saltwater of academics. I drank it for four years of college, two years of engineering graduate school, and three years of seminary. It was a nine-year saltwater binge.

Passing on Grade-A Water

Although the Bible never speaks directly about drinking saltwater, one passage soundly captures a similar idea. In the second chapter of the book of Jeremiah, the prophet scolds the tribe of Judah—a group of God's people living in what is now modern Palestine. He says this:

> This is what the LORD says: ... "My people have committed two sins: They have forsaken me, the spring of living water, and have dug their own cisterns, broken cisterns that cannot hold water." (Jeremiah 2 v 5, 13)

A little background to Jeremiah's imagery here. During Jeremiah's time, the Judeans had three customary water sources. *Grade-A water* came from springs or streams—fresh running water often called "living water." *Grade-B water* came from the ground and was typically stored in wells. *Grade-F water* was found in cisterns—shallow plaster-coated cavities in the ground. The water in these cisterns was often nothing more than dirty runoff water covered with bugs. It certainly wasn't ideal for drinking.

To make matters worse, the Judeans' cisterns were cracked, leaking water into the surrounding ground until they were empty, with only dead bugs remaining.

What point is Jeremiah making here? First, the Judeans are thirsty. Not physically thirsty—*spiritually* thirsty. They have the same nagging thirst you and I have—a thirst for paradise lost. Second, they're trying to quench it apart from God. They've completely abandoned him. They've placed their hope in people, places, and practices that are spiritually empty—as empty as cracked cisterns. These people, places, and practices are also impure, tainted, and polluted—as polluted as nasty bug water. And just as drinking polluted bug water leads to greater physical dehydration (think diarrhea and vomiting), their *spiritual* dehydration is only worsening.

As if this isn't bad enough, the Judeans are also suffering a massive communal hangover after drinking "cistern water." Their nation is in decay. Their economy is in shambles. Their political system is corrupt. Morality has plummeted. Enemy nations are after them. War is the new normal. A dark cloud is hovering over Judah.

Jeremiah said the Judeans were drinking from cracked cisterns. I say they were drinking saltwater. We're making the same point.

Mixed Drinks

You might be asking a question: Can saltwater be mixed? Can we be sipping multiple forms at the same time? And can we do so without even knowing it? Absolutely. Here's an example:

Between my first and second years of seminary, I spent a summer living and working with drug addicts at the New York City Rescue Mission. I met Victor one hot Tuesday morning. When he entered the mission, he'd been off heroin for three days and was beginning a lengthy and painful detox process. His body was shaking. He was sweating profusely. He couldn't stop scratching his face. His eyes were bloodshot—the result of not sleeping for days. He was terrified of everybody and became angry at the drop of a hat. He was ashamed of himself and yet defended himself incessantly. He was unhealthy inside and out.

When I met Victor, his saltwater of choice seemed clear—heroin. He'd been drinking—actually guzzling—it for years. He'd developed an almost insurmountable tolerance to the drug and was suffering from near-death withdrawal symptoms. He was a textbook heroin addict. It took all of fifteen seconds to figure this out.

But heroin wasn't the only form of saltwater Victor was drinking. He was mixing it with a less obvious form—the saltwater of *image*. Victor was obsessed with his reputation. He craved appearing strong, put together, and respectable in others' eyes. How did he obtain this form of saltwater? How did he gain human approval? He lied. Victor was a *compulsive* liar.

Victor's lying problem was on full display just four days into his stay when he was granted a two-hour pass to visit a family member. Upon returning to the mission, the emotionally, physically, and spiritually dilapidated man was suddenly smiling and energetic. He was joyfully unloading boxes off a food-delivery truck, telling jokes, and laughing involuntarily.

This was terrible news. Victor was no longer in detox.

When I asked him why he felt so much better, Victor stared me in the face and lied. "God healed me." God healed him? Nope. God didn't heal him. The fresh heroin in his system "healed" him. Why did Victor lie? He didn't want to disappoint me. He wanted my approval. He wanted to preserve his image.

Eventually, the mission staff caught on and confronted Victor. Predictably, he took another sip of saltwater, denied their accusations in an effort to save face, packed up his stuff, and walked out of the mission.

He then went on a four-week heroin bender.

When Victor again reached rock bottom, he returned to the mission, begged for re-entry, and was given a second chance at recovery. Over the next six weeks, I grew closer to Victor and learned more about his image addiction and compulsive lying habits. In our daily conversations, he flaunted lies about his past relationships, sexual exploits, and financial prosperity. He told tales of friendships with A-list celebrities. He bragged about imaginary college degrees. He spit out lists of career accomplishments that would impress Steve Jobs. The scary thing? He believed his lies. He'd lied so much he was convinced his fairy tales were true. He lived in a world in which he was the hero of every story.

Soon I realized that Victor's arrival at the New York City Rescue Mission wasn't the consequence of him drinking straight shots of heroin saltwater. He was sipping a mixed drink—part heroin saltwater, part image saltwater. Consuming *this* concoction led Victor to homelessness. It burnt bridges with his family, friends, co-workers, bosses, and even fellow addicts—anybody who might be willing to take him in. It extinguished all flickering flames of trust in those he most wanted to impress. His part-heroin, part-image saltwater beverage was the poison that put Victor on the streets.

Like Victor's, our unique saltwater forms are often hard to identify at first. And they typically show up in muddled mixed drinks.

Appreciating Saltwater

It's easy to read these stories and conclude that saltwater is inherently evil. But is it?

No. Let's first look at the literal saltwater that surrounded Louie Zamperini. In many ways, the 187-quintillion-gallon

Pacific Ocean was a friend to him. It provided a relatively soft landing for him. It disinfected his scrapes, sores, and blisters. It reduced the swelling in his badly bruised legs and cooled his sunburnt skin. It even housed the fish he caught and ate. And for those of us who aren't stranded in the middle of the ocean, it can also be beneficial. Saltwater can be used to soften our skin, store our contact lenses, and fill our pools. It can help cure athlete's foot, laryngitis, eczema, sore throats, and toothaches. At the very least, it can be a thing of beauty, as shown by elevated real-estate prices for ocean-view properties.

In the same way, the metaphorical saltwater that I'm describing isn't inherently evil. Money isn't evil. Sex isn't evil. Control, comfort, busyness, people, food, and works aren't evil. Not even heroin—occasionally prescribed by doctors for pain management—is fundamentally evil. When used and enjoyed for its intended purpose—appreciated as God designed it to be appreciated—saltwater is a very good thing.

We just weren't meant to drink it.

God's Wonderful Alternative

What should we drink instead? The answer's right there in the Jeremiah passage:

> My people have committed two sins: They have forsaken
> me, **the spring of living water**, and have dug their
> own cisterns, broken cisterns that cannot hold water.
> (Jeremiah 2 v 13, bold text mine)

God tells us the drink that will quench our thirst. It's called living water. And it's offered to all. Sit tight and I'll explain this mysterious beverage in chapter 4.

In the meantime, let's explore in greater detail what happens when we sip saltwater instead...

3. THE SALTWATER CYCLE

$3.6 million.

This was Sam Polk's bonus in 2010—his final year as a hedge-fund trader on Wall Street.

Just eight years earlier, he was a broke college student, a daily drinker, and a frequent user of cocaine, Ritalin, and ecstasy. He'd been arrested twice. He'd been suspended from Columbia University for burglary. He'd been fired from an Internet company for fighting. His future looked bleak.

Somehow, Polk smooth-talked his way into a position with a major Wall Street bank out of college. It was the dream job for a young man with a knack for math and a belief that money could solve his problems. His first-year bonus was $40,000. He was ecstatic. For the first time, he could withdraw money from an ATM without checking his balance.

Polk moved up the corporate ladder rapidly and his bonuses grew from five to seven figures. After four years, a competing bank offered him a salary of $1.75 million. He turned it down. Yes, it was more money than his mom had earned in her entire life as a nurse practitioner. But it wasn't enough for Polk. Instead, he left to work for a hedge fund, where he believed he could make more.

He was right.

In 2010, he got a $3.6 million bonus. In a *New York Times* article entitled "For the Love of Money," he shared his response to the bonus:

> *I was angry because it wasn't big enough. I was 30 years old, had no children to raise, no debts to pay, no philanthropic goal in mind. I wanted more money for exactly the same reason an alcoholic needs another drink: I was addicted.*

How did Polk get to this point? How did he go from a dirt-poor college student to a ravenous wealth-addict in just eight years?

He was drinking saltwater. The form? Money. In 2002, he took his first sip. Over the next eight years, the sips became deeper and more frequent. By 2010, he was gulping it down and couldn't stop. He was completely addicted to it.

How does this happen? How do we become addicted to saltwater?

I call it **the saltwater cycle**. It consists of three steps, repeats itself endlessly, and eventually leads to hell both in this life and the life to come.

1. We listen to a lie
2. We drink
3. We suffer

Saltwater Cycle Step 1: We Listen to a Lie

The first step in the saltwater cycle is somewhat passive. We listen to a lie. The lie is that saltwater can quench our thirst for paradise. Who spreads it? The liars are threefold: the world, the flesh, and the devil.

Liar #1: The World

The world, as I'm using it here, refers to the people and cultural institutions teaching us how to think and what to believe. It includes politicians, professors, artists, athletes, clients, counselors, models, musicians, producers, publishers, authors, actors, friends, family, and *anybody* else out there who is shaping our values and directing our hopes. Put simply, it's the society we live in.

It has one primary way to spread the lie that saltwater can quench our thirst for paradise—the media. It lies through the written media in the form of books, magazines, websites, newspapers, and blogs. It lies through the spoken media in the form of radio shows, podcasts, songs, and everyday conversations. It lies through social media in the form of tweets, status updates, and photo posts. It lies through television in the form of 22-minute pictures of life as it rarely exists. The world is wholeheartedly committed to spreading the lie that saltwater can give us paradise, and does it through every form of media available.

Liar #2: The Flesh

Not only does the world lie to us, but we also lie to ourselves. We dupe, deceive, and delude ourselves into thinking that paradise is available in saltwater. More accurately, the liar within us is what the Bible calls our "flesh" (Romans 8 v 5-8). The flesh is the part of us that doesn't want anything to do with God. For many of us, the flesh is king. It rules us. It dominates our thoughts, actions, emotions, and motives. And it deceives us. It tells us that things of this world can free us from our troubles, trials, and toils. It persuades us that people, places, objects, and feelings can liberate us from all suffering. Like a siren luring sailors to their death, our flesh sings a tantalizing song of fake paradise via saltwater. All of us hear the song. Some of us sing along.

Liar #3: The Devil

I introduced the third liar back in chapter one. Call him the devil. Call him Satan. Call him whatever you'd like. No matter what name you attach to him, he's God's enemy. If you don't think he's real, then he has you right where he wants you. According to the Bible, he's prowling around like a roaring lion, looking for somebody to devour (1 Peter 5 v 8). He has a team of spiritual forces working alongside him, and they're all lying to you too. They're taunting, seducing, and tempting you—whispering into your ear that you can find true joy in this world apart from God. They're seducing you with the fib that saltwater can save you.

There you have it. The three-headed monster. The unholy trinity. The world, the flesh, and the devil. They're lying to you. They're trying to convince you that you're in the drink. They're vowing to quench the insatiable thirst within your soul. They're pledging relief from the suffering that has stalked you from birth. They're promising paradise by saltwater.

Saltwater Cycle Step 2: We Drink

1. We listen to a lie

3. We suffer   2. We drink

After listening to the lie that saltwater can give us paradise, we have two options. Option one is to reject the lie and pour it out. Adam and Eve could have left the forbidden fruit on the tree. My father could have dumped out his beer. Victor could have told the truth. I could have put down my pencil. Polk could have given away his money. We can *all* reject the lie that saltwater can give us paradise. We can all pour it out.

The second option is to believe the lie. And drink.

Most of us choose option two.

But what does this mean? What does it mean to *drink* saltwater? First, I must define two terms—*gift* and *god*.

Gift

When you think of a gift, you probably imagine a box with a bow on it or an envelope with cash in it. But I'm defining a gift as *any good thing given to us from God*. Gifts include money, movies, sex, sleep, family, friendships, computers, clothes, books, boats, emotions, entertainment, jobs, jokes, shoes, shakes, vacations, vocations... *any* good thing from God. We're meant to enjoy gifts and use them for their intended purposes. Nothing more. Nothing less.

Just like saltwater.

Now I'll define a second, more complicated term: *god*.

god

Notice that I'm using a small g here. I'm not talking about the Creator of the universe, who we call God. I'm talking about the created things in and around us that take the place of God. The Bible calls them idols.

They're the people, places, and things that rule our lives. They hijack our hearts. They steal our souls. We put our hopes in them. We fill our minds with them. We offer our bodies to them. Ultimately, we worship them.

How do you know if something is a god in your life? Ask yourself a series of test questions. Who do you adore *way* too much? What do you obsess about? What do you fantasize about? What are you terrified of losing? What do you *Need* with a capital N? What do you spend way too much time doing? What is your go-to escape in the midst of suffering? In times of silence, where does your mind naturally gravitate? What gives you meaning and purpose? What gives your life security? Where do you put your trust when life is scary? What do you dwell on? How do you find inner peace? What do you spend way too much money on? What defines you?

What do you worship? That is your god.

Ironically, perhaps the greatest indicator of a god in your life is hatred in your heart toward something else. In other words, when you're demonizing something, it typically means you're idolizing its counterpart. For example, a woman with judgment in her heart toward obese people is likely worshiping the gods of fitness, beauty, discipline, and self-control. A man who looks down on minimum-wage workers is likely worshiping the gods of power, achievement, and professional advancement. A toddler who resents his friend with a shiny new tricycle is likely worshiping the god of material possessions (yes, it starts that early).

If we're demonizing something, we're usually idolizing something else.

Now that I've defined these two terms—gift and god—I can define what it means to drink saltwater:

Drinking saltwater means turning a gift from God into a god.

It means looking for salvation in something that was never meant to save us. It means deifying something we were merely supposed to enjoy. It means turning a good thing into an ultimate thing. It means worshiping something that was never meant to be worshiped.

Drinking saltwater is what the Bible calls *idolatry*.

And we're all guilty of it. We're all idolaters. We all drink saltwater.

So why is the title of this book **Sipping** *Saltwater*? Why not **Drinking** *Saltwater*? Because our idolatry is usually subtle. We're not typically guzzling, pounding, inhaling, or slamming down saltwater like my dad, Victor, me, or Polk in my previous illustrations. We're often not even drinking it in the general sense of the word "drink." We're usually sipping it. We're taking slow, subtle, quiet, gentle, and measured tastes. We're placing it to our lips and allowing small amounts to enter our mouths. We're savoring it and slowly swallowing. Sometimes we're sipping it subconsciously—we don't even realize we're doing it. But God sees our sips. Our tiny little sips. Every single one. And he takes each sip very seriously.

Saltwater Cycle Step 3: We Suffer

Let's go back to Louie. If he'd swallowed saltwater from the Pacific, it would have made him thirstier and left him with a brutal hangover. The same thing happens when we drink saltwater—when we turn gifts from God into gods. Not only do these gods fail to deliver on their promise to hydrate our souls, they leave us thirstier than we were before, with biting hangovers as a result. We feel guilt, shame, anger, fear, sadness, grief, hopelessness, sorrow, distress, dejection, and gloom. Our hearts hurt. Our emotions tumble. We ache on the inside. Our relationships suffer on the outside. We suffer spiritual pain. Soul pain.

How do we respond?

Like an alcoholic with a debilitating hangover, we promise ourselves we'll never drink again.

But just as alcohol hangovers eventually wear off, so do our saltwater hangovers. The soul pain loses its edge as time passes. The guilt and shame diminish. The internal ache subsides. The agony dissipates, and we find ourselves thirsty once again. *Thirstier.*

And the cycle repeats.

We listen to the same lies from the world, the flesh, and the devil. We again believe the lies. We sip more saltwater—usually in greater quantity to satisfy our intensified thirst. We become more spiritually dehydrated. We experience worse soul pain. It wears off. We're more parched than ever. And the saltwater cycle starts over.

Pretty soon we're no longer sipping. We're gulping. And with every trip through the saltwater cycle, our gulps become deeper and more frequent. Our tolerance to saltwater grows. Our withdrawal symptoms worsen. After enough saltwater cycles, we need saltwater just to feel normal.

And we're officially addicted.

But that's not the worst part...

Where Does the Saltwater Cycle Lead?

The end result of the saltwater cycle isn't just addiction. If we're unwilling to spit out our saltwater and escape the cycle, the end result is hell.

A parable from the Gospel of Luke (16 v 19-31) illustrates this scary point. The two main characters of the story are a nameless tycoon—a biblical version of Sam Polk—and a man named Lazarus. The rich man wears purple—a sign of great wealth—and lives in luxury. Lazarus, on the other hand, begs at the gate of the rich man's estate, while wild dogs lick his open sores. The rich man knows Lazarus by name but ignores him. He could give him food, shelter, and medical care. But there's no indication that he does anything for him.

When the rich man dies, he receives a proper burial. Lazarus doesn't. But after death, their fortunes are reversed. Lazarus goes to heaven and the rich man goes to hell, where he'll spend eternity in torment. When the rich man looks up and sees Abraham and Lazarus standing side by side, he calls to Abraham:

> Father Abraham, have pity on me and send Lazarus to dip the tip of his finger in water and cool my tongue, because I am in agony in this fire. (Luke 16 v 24)

Abraham's got bad news for the rich man.

> Son, remember that in your lifetime you received your good things, while Lazarus received bad things, but now

he is comforted here and you are in agony. And besides
all this, between us and you a great chasm has been
set in place, so that those who want to go from here to
you cannot, nor can anyone cross over from there to us.
(Luke 16 v 25-26)

I understand nobody likes to talk about hell. I certainly don't.
But this story sends a clear message. First, hell is real. Second,
it's the destination of anyone whose life is defined by saltwater
addiction like the rich man (his saltwater presumably being
money and possessions). If we're unwilling to escape the
accelerating merry-go-round of the saltwater cycle, we'll end
up with this rich man on the wrong side of the unbridgeable
chasm between heaven and hell. Forever.

Hope

It's easy to read this chapter and feel dejected, if not terrified.
If, like me, you're struggling with saltwater addiction (and yes,
you probably are), are you doomed to hell now and in the life
to come?

No. There's hope.

But the hope for freedom doesn't lie in a psychological
technique, a pill, or a self-help strategy. It doesn't lie in
willpower, intelligence, or skill. It certainly doesn't lie in
drinking more saltwater.

It lies in a *person*.

4. LIVING WATER

In 2005, Brittni Ruiz became a porn star.

She was beautiful, insecure, abused, and unloved—the perfect credentials for an aspiring porn actress. Under the professional name Jenna Presley, she started at 18 and hit the ground running in search of the love she'd lacked her entire life. She worked as many as 60 consecutive days shooting up to three sex scenes per day. She starred in more than 275 films over seven years. In 2006, she was runner-up on *Jenna's American Sex Star*—a reality TV show hosted by porn legend Jenna Jameson. In 2010, *Maxim* magazine named her one of the "top twelve hottest porn stars in the world." Producers coveted her. Men worshiped her. She was not only loved—she had *fans*. Life was good, right?

Nope.

Like most porn stars, Ruiz became depressed. In her words, she turned into an "emotionless rubber Barbie doll." To cope, she self-medicated with alcohol, cocaine, and heroin. She cut her wrists. She tried suicide multiple times. She wanted out of the porn world but, like most in the industry, had no idea how to leave.

Until November 2012.

What happened? How did she find the courage to step off the set and leave her flourishing yet toxic porn career? What ultimately liberated Ruiz from the enslaving power of the industry? Where did she find freedom?

She found it in Jesus Christ.

Let's meet him.

The Story of Insatia

In the fourth chapter of the Gospel of John, we read the story of the famous and nameless "woman at the well." I'll call her Insatia. She lived over 2,000 years ago in Samaria, located in modern Jordan. At the base of a well she has an encounter with Jesus. Here's a snippet of the story:

> Now he [Jesus] had to go through Samaria. So he came to a town in Samaria called Sychar, near the plot of ground Jacob had given to his son Joseph. Jacob's well was there, and Jesus, tired as he was from the journey, sat down by the well. It was about noon.
>
> When a Samaritan woman came to draw water, Jesus said to her, "Will you give me a drink?" (His disciples had gone into the town to buy food.)
>
> The Samaritan woman said to him, "You are a Jew and I am a Samaritan woman. How can you ask me for a drink?" (For Jews do not associate with Samaritans.)
>
> Jesus answered her, "If you knew the gift of God and who it is that asks you for a drink, you would have asked him and he would have given you living water."

"Sir," the woman said, "you have nothing to draw with and the well is deep. Where can you get this living water? Are you greater than our father Jacob, who gave us the well and drank from it himself, as did also his sons and his livestock?"

Jesus answered, "Everyone who drinks this water will be thirsty again, but whoever drinks the water I give them will never thirst. Indeed, the water I give them will become in them a spring of water welling up to eternal life."

The woman said to him, "Sir, give me this water so that I won't get thirsty and have to keep coming here to draw water."

He told her, "Go, call your husband and come back."

"I have no husband," she replied.

Jesus said to her, "You are right when you say you have no husband. The fact is, you have had five husbands, and the man you now have is not your husband. What you have just said is quite true." (John 4 v 4-18)

What's Jesus doing in this little scene? Three things. First, he's redirecting Insatia's attention away from her surface-level problem toward her deeper problem. She thinks her problem is physical. He's saying it's spiritual. She thinks it's a dry bucket. He's saying it's a dry heart. In other words, although she never asks for it, Jesus is opening her eyes to her most significant ailment in life—her unquenched spiritual thirst.

Second, as if he'd been following Insatia her entire life, Jesus is exposing her futile attempts to quench this thirst with saltwater. Her form of choice? Her five previous husbands and current sexual escapades hint that she's sipping the saltwater of human love. Just like Brittni Ruiz.

Finally, he's offering her a better drink. He's offering her *living water*.

The Gift of the Spirit

Insatia was confused by Jesus' offer of living water. She doesn't get the metaphor. What is this curious beverage? We have to read ahead in John's Gospel to find out. In John 7, Jesus stands up in the middle of a Jewish festival and gives his audience a bold invitation:

> Let anyone who is thirsty come to me and drink.
> Whoever believes in me, as Scripture has said, rivers of living water will flow from within them. (John 7 v 37-38)

In the next verse, John clears up what Jesus means:

> By this he meant the Spirit, whom those who believed in him were later to receive. (John 7 v 39)

John tells us that living water is the Spirit of God. It's this Spirit—commonly referred to as the Holy Spirit—who frees us from our saltwater addictions. How? First, he opens our eyes and convicts us of our bondage to the drink (John 16 v 8). He then strengthens us to spit it out—to repent of our futile attempts to find paradise outside of God (Ephesians 3 v 16). Finally, he purifies our hearts so we'll never want to drink saltwater again (2 Thessalonians 2 v 13). The Spirit replaces our affections for saltwater with affections for Christ.

What else do we learn about living water from this story? At least five things.

The One Source

First, living water comes from Jesus. He's the source. Not Allah, Buddha, Mohammed, Joseph Smith, or any other false god or prophet out there. You won't find it in Hinduism, Judaism, Buddhism, Mormonism, or any world religion but Christianity. You can't get it in yoga. Or positive thinking. Or "spirituality." It can't be found in long-distance running, organic food, Pilates, pets, gadgets, sex, marriage, children, or work. Living water comes from Jesus. *He's* the source.

Offered to Anybody

Second, it's offered to *anybody*. If we examine Insatia's credentials, she's the most unlikely of candidates. She's a Samaritan—seen as a religious outcast by the Jews in Jesus' day. She's also a woman—a mark of inferiority to many in the male-dominated first century. Finally, she's alone—a probable sign she's been shunned by the other women, who would gather water during the cooler morning hours. By religious, gender, moral, and social standards, Insatia's a second-class citizen. If living water is offered to *her*, it's offered to anybody. Including me. And you.

Received by Faith

Third, we receive living water by believing in Jesus. Not by following rules. Or attending church services. Or serving at homeless shelters. Or being raised in religious homes. We can only receive living water by believing in Jesus. What must we believe about him?

- That he's God—fully God.
- That he became a person like you and me—fully man.
- That he was tempted like us to sip saltwater daily and yet never drank a drop. *Not one drop.*

- That his reward for such a sinless life was death on a cross.
- That his death paid the penalty for our repeated trips to our saltwater fountains.
- That he rose from the dead, is seated at the right hand of the Father, and will one day come back to restore the paradise that was lost in the Garden of Eden.

We must believe that Jesus is the Savior of the world. Not just a good man. Not just a good teacher. Not just a prophet. Not just one of many paths to God. We must believe that Jesus is the only true God, and submit our lives to him, if we are to receive living water.

True Quenching

Fourth, living water *will* satisfy you. Jesus tells Insatia that those who drink it *will never thirst* (John 4 v 14). Never. The apostle Paul explains what a quenched thirst looks like—what we'll experience when we're consumed with the Spirit of God. He says we'll enjoy the "fruit of the Spirit."

> But the fruit of the Spirit is love, joy, peace, forbearance, kindness, goodness, faithfulness, gentleness and self-control. Against such things there is no law.
> (Galatians 5 v 22-23)

Take a moment to think about this list. Can you imagine having these virtues? All the time? Can you imagine enjoying unfleeting love? Delighting in unconditional joy and impenetrable peace? Having limitless patience—what Paul calls forbearance? Experiencing instinctive kindness and untainted selflessness—what Paul calls goodness? Having unwavering faith in God? Being gentle and self-controlled whatever the circumstance?

Just for a second—think about such a life. *Perfect* love, joy, peace, forbearance, kindness, goodness, faithfulness, gentleness, and self-control. *Always*. Doesn't it sound satisfying? Doesn't it sound like paradise? It is. And if you drink living water, paradise can be yours. Your thirst for paradise *can* be quenched.

The Promise of Eternal Life

Fifth, drinking living water results in eternal life. When we die, paradise lost will become paradise found. We won't suffer the hellish fate of the rich man from the previous chapter. Instead, we'll be with Lazarus and God in heaven. Forever. No more suffering. No more pain. It will be better than anything you could ever imagine. Better than the best day of your life. Better than sex. Better than chocolate. Better than the best vacation you've ever taken. Better than anything this world could offer. You'll be with God in paradise. Forever.

To summarize these five points about living water (which is the Spirit of God): its source is Jesus; it's offered to anybody; we receive it through faith in Christ; it quenches our thirst for paradise lost; and it results in eternal life.

It's the greatest gift that Jesus could have offered to Insatia. It's the greatest gift he's offering to you.

Let me tell you about two people who chose to receive this gift. I've already introduced both. We'll start with Louie Zamperini.

Back to Louie

As Louie floated on the Pacific for 47 days, his only chance of getting drinkable water was from rain. For three weeks he collected enough to survive. But then the rain stopped. Six days into the drought, Louie recognized he wouldn't survive much longer without water. So he prayed. He prayed that if God quenched his thirst, he'd dedicate his life to him.

The next day, rain came down. Louie stayed alive and kept floating.

Eventually he found land—an island occupied by the Japanese. He became a prisoner of war and was tortured for the next two years. He lived in a tiny cell infested with flies, mosquitos, and feces. He ate only seaweed, depleting his body to 65 lbs (30 kg). His guards spit on him, beat him, and injected him with experimental medicines. One officer known as "the Bird" became obsessed with breaking him down. He struck him across the face regularly with a leather belt—steel buckle and all. After two years, Louie was almost dead.

But then good news arrived.

In August 1945, Japan surrendered. The war was over. Louie returned home. He was wined, dined, and heralded not only as a former Olympian, but now as a war hero. His celebrity status grew. As did his ego. He was on top of the world.

But then post-traumatic stress disorder set in. Louie started having nightmares. Every night he dreamt of the Bird beating him. One night he woke up strangling his wife Cynthia, thinking she was the Bird. The dreams didn't subside over time—they got worse. Louie was in the greatest fight of his life. He responded by sipping saltwater in the form of alcohol. It provided temporary comfort but predictably led to addiction. Instead of the Japanese, alcohol became his enemy. His marriage fell apart. Cynthia threatened to divorce him.

But then everything changed. Cynthia invited him to a tent revival. He snickered at the evangelist's message the first night and walked out. The second night, however, was different. During the message, something clicked in Louie.

He remembered his promise to God.

Two years earlier, Louie had promised that if God quenched his thirst with rain, he'd dedicate his life to him. He did that evening. He drank Jesus' living water and became a Christian. His life changed forever. And I mean *forever*.

Miraculously, he became free from the bondage of alcohol. The nightmares stopped. His anger toward his Japanese captors ceased. The Spirit of God entered his heart and he found peace. This peace led him to do something absurd. Not long after he started drinking living water as a Christian, Louie returned to the land where his nightmares began. This time he went to a completely different prison—one filled with over 850 Japanese war criminals. He met his former guards there. And he forgave them. All of them.

Even the Bird.

Louie died in 2014 at 97 years old. His living water has now welled up to eternal life.

Back to Brittni

What about Brittni Ruiz, the former porn star? How did she gain the strength to leave the industry?

She also drank living water.

In the midst of her emotional breakdown, Ruiz met members of Triple-X Church at the Exxxotica Expo—a porn convention in New Jersey. The church pleaded with her to choose Jesus over her porn career. The penny dropped. Her heart melted. She spit out the saltwater of human love and found divine love in Jesus. For the first time in her life, she was free.

In an interview with a British newspaper, she stated, "I never found love in my life and was looking for it in all the wrong places. I finally found the unconditional love of God. And I will never go back."

Living water was Ruiz's only hope for freedom from the porn industry. In it she found healing. She found love. She found home.

And you can too.

We taste Thee, O Thou Living Bread,
And long to feast upon Thee still:
We drink of Thee, the Fountainhead,
And thirst our souls from Thee to fill.

—Bernard of Clairvaux: "Jesus, Thou Joy of Loving Hearts"

5. WATER FOUNTAINS

"If you gave me several million years, there would be nothing that did not grow in beauty if it were surrounded by water."

Jan Erik Vold, *What All the World Knows*

"We're on the brink of divorce and you're our last hope."

As a marriage counselor, I hear this often. When Ben said it, he wasn't exaggerating. He'd been cheating on his wife, Carrie, for over a decade and she'd finally caught him. The twist? His affairs were with men. *Dozens* of men. Carrie caught him while innocently perusing his e-mail for a receipt. After the revelation, Ben admitted he'd been addicted to homosexual hookups since their honeymoon. After each sexual encounter, he'd justify it as "not real cheating" since it was with a man. He'd use a similar mind game to justify his addiction to homosexual pornography.

Aside from the cheating, Ben was failing as a husband in other areas. He rarely talked to Carrie, and when he did he was short and combative. Date nights consisted of quarterly dinners out with him paying far more attention to his phone than his wife. He lived an independent life in the house—working, sleeping, and entertaining himself in the basement while Carrie took care of their three children upstairs. He didn't give her birthday presents. He didn't have sex with her. He didn't eat with her. He didn't do anything with her. They were distant roommates at best.

Why do I share this story?

Ben's marriage was falling apart for two reasons. First, he was pursuing other lovers—gay men. Second, he *wasn't pursuing Carrie*. He wasn't cultivating their sacred relationship.

It's the same with us and God. On the one hand, we pursue other lovers in the form of idols. We turn gifts from God into gods. We sip saltwater. On the other hand, we *don't pursue him*. We don't drink living water. We don't cultivate our sacred relationship with Jesus. That's what this chapter is about—fostering our relationship with Christ. How do we do it? What are the practical steps we must take to drink his living water? What must we do to experience his satisfying presence in our lives? How do we enjoy Spirit-filled lives drenched in living water?

Let's look at how the first Christians did it.

The First Church Ever

In the second chapter of the book of Acts, the author Luke paints a picture of the first Christian community guzzling down living water together:

> They devoted themselves to the apostles' teaching and to fellowship, to the breaking of bread and to prayer. Everyone was filled with awe at the many wonders and signs performed by the apostles. All the believers were together and had everything in common. They sold

property and possessions to give to anyone who had need. Every day they continued to meet together in the temple courts. They broke bread in their homes and ate together with glad and sincere hearts, praising God and enjoying the favor of all the people. And the Lord added to their number daily those who were being saved.
(Acts 2 v 42-47)

A little background to this scene. At this point, Jesus had lived, died, and been resurrected from the dead. After he was raised, he made several public appearances during a 40-day period before finally ascending to be with the Father in heaven. The apostles were then filled with the Holy Spirit for the first time, Peter gave the first Christian sermon, and 3,000 people became Christians. They became the first church *ever*. And this is what they did.

If we dissect the passage, we see at least six ways the first believers drank living water. I'm calling these "water fountains"—delivery mechanisms for living water. It's important not to confuse these water fountains with the Fountain of living water—Jesus himself. He's the source, supplier, and spring from which all living water flows. These fountains are simply the means through which Jesus delivers living water to us. They're ways to experience the Spirit of God.

Devoted to the Bible

The first water fountain is Scripture. The passage says the early church "devoted themselves to the apostles' teaching." Where can we find this teaching now that the apostles are no longer alive? In the Bible. Everything we need to know about Jesus is in God's word. As we read it, we learn about Jesus' infinite love, grace, wisdom, patience, justice, faithfulness, holiness, and knowledge. We experience the passion, power, and purity that make him who he is. Our hearts, minds, and souls are illuminated by his presence. We're transformed.

When I meet somebody who feels distant from Jesus, I ask one question: "What are you learning about him in the Bible lately?" I typically get a blank stare. In other words, they're not reading the Bible. It makes sense, then, that they're distant from Christ. How can they feel close to somebody they don't know? Without spending consistent time in the Bible, Jesus turns into a divine concept—not the personal God who interacts personally with you. Not the God who heals, comforts, and calms. Not the God who erases our guilt, shame, anger, and anxiety. Not the God who lived a sinless life, died a horrific death, was raised from the dead, and will one day return to usher in heaven for eternity. Not the source of living water.

Open the Bible. Every day. No, I mean it. Every. Single. Day. Learn about Jesus. See what he does to you as you learn about him. See how your heart changes as he speaks to you. See how your sin decreases and your love for him increases. See how you're transformed. See how your thirst is quenched.

Quality Time with Other Christians

The second water fountain is fellowship—spending quality time with other Christians. Acts 2 says the early church met together *every day*, eating meals and gathering in the temple courts. Why did they do this? Why did they reject individualism and pursue such a communal lifestyle?

They needed it to survive and grow.

Let's say you cut off your finger. What would happen to it? It would die. Why? It would be separated from the rest of your body with no way to receive the nourishment necessary to live. Christians—who Paul calls members of the "body of Christ" (Ephesians 5 v 30)—are no different. If we're separated from Christ's body, we die spiritually. We need the spiritual nourishment that people provide. We need each other for support, refreshment, insight, wisdom, comfort, companionship, help, and hope. We need role models—people to learn from and emulate. We need men and women observing us. We need people coaching, challenging, and sharpening us. We need accountability. We need people. They're *living* water fountains.

Talking to Jesus

The third water fountain is prayer. If Scripture is how God speaks to us, prayer is how we speak back to God. It's our opportunity to share our hearts with him—to ask him questions and talk openly about the good, bad, and ugly of our lives. It can be formal or informal, pre-written or freestyle, public or private, spoken, thought, sung, written, rapped, shouted, whispered, chanted... you name it. We're all wired differently and we all pray differently.

I'd like to share a prayer format that nicely combines structure and spontaneity. I use it often. It's called ACTOR.

- **Adoration.** First, I focus on the qualities and characteristics that make God *God*. I admire him for who the Bible says he is. I work extra hard not to turn this into a time of thanksgiving—that's two steps ahead.

- **Confession.** In light of who God is, who am I? I'm sinful. I take time to admit that I'm a saltwater-sipper and identify the forms I'm sipping. I grieve over my saltwater addictions—not to earn God's approval, but to appropriately feel their weight and ugliness.

- **Thanksgiving.** I then share gratitude for what God has done for me. He's sent Jesus to live, die, and pay the penalty for my saltwater addictions. He's given me living water to sustain, satisfy, and save me. He's done everything revealed in the Bible and so much more. He supplies every one of my needs. He allows me to suffer and uses my suffering to shape me. He doesn't always give me what I ask for, but he gives me what I *would* ask for if I knew what he knows.

- **Others.** I then shift my focus to others—people close to me and people I've never met. What do they need? How are they hurting? Where are they struggling? Are they distant from God? Are they distant from friends, family, and fellowship? My goal is to pray for them as fervently as I would pray for myself.

- **Requests.** Finally, I ask God to bless me. I ask boldly and don't hold back. However, I like to end with the same disclaimer Jesus used when asking the Father to remove his suffering prior to his crucifixion: *"yet not my will, but yours be done"* (Luke 22 v 42).

As you're praying, you're drinking living water. Do so often. Do so fervently. Do so knowing God is listening. And answering. And quenching your thirst in the process.

Life-Giving Generosity

The fourth water fountain is generosity. The passage says the early church "had everything in common" and "sold property and possessions to give to anyone who had need." How is generosity a water fountain? How does selflessness enable us to fall more in love with Jesus? An illustration and some words from Jesus provide the answer.

Sharon never wanted children. She wasn't opposed to marriage, but the thought of taking care of a baby, then a toddler, and then eventually (gulp!) a teenager was less than appealing. She got married in her mid-20s and her husband was equally committed to marriage without children for life.

Of course, she got pregnant two months after their wedding.

After giving birth, Sharon's life was no longer her own—it belonged to her son, Nolan. Her days consisted of feeding him, bathing him, changing him, comforting him, calming him, entertaining him, shopping for him, washing his clothes, cooking for him, reading to him, and exposing him to the world. Her nights consisted of short naps interrupted by feeding sessions, diaper changes, and triage care for his emergencies. Her life was all about Nolan.

One would have expected her to despise him.

Nope. She fell in love with him.

As Sharon poured her time, energy, resources, money, labor, and knowledge into Nolan, something in her heart changed. She became attached to her son. Her love for him grew. Jesus tells us why in the Gospel of Matthew, where he says, "Where your treasure is, there your heart will be also" (Matthew 6 v 21). In other words, our hearts follow our resources. Generosity toward people results in love for those people. Sharon's affections for Nolan increased every time she laid down her life for him.

But wait—didn't I say that generosity toward others enables us to love *Jesus* more? Yes. Later in the Gospel of Matthew, Jesus explains why. He says, *"Whatever you did for one of the least of these ... you did for me"* (Matthew 25 v 40). He's saying that the horizontal sacrifices of Christians are also *vertical* sacrifices. When we're generous toward others, we're being generous toward *him*. And from Matthew 6 v 21, we see that as we're generous toward him—as we pour our treasure into him—our hearts will also attach to him.

Putting it all together, we fall more in love with Jesus as we give ourselves to others. It's a beautiful roundabout way to drink living water.

Everyday Praise

The fifth water fountain is praise. The passage says that the early Christians were "praising God and enjoying the favor of all the people" (Acts 2 v 47). Of course, we can praise God in church every Sunday. But I'd like to focus on "everyday praise." How do you praise God on a Tuesday morning when you're brushing your teeth? How do you praise him at 3pm on a Wednesday afternoon while working? What does praise look like during the 166 weekly hours when church isn't in session?

I'm a runner. I've been one since my early 20s. I've run a couple of marathons and a handful of other races. But my favorite run isn't a race—it's the 8-mile jog I take alone every Saturday afternoon. It's a time when I connect with God. It's a time when I listen to music about God, think about God, pray to God, and praise God. I understand that an 8-mile run would be the *worst* time for many people to connect with God. Not for me. When I hit the pavement, praise is instinctive.

What's your version of my Saturday jog? Perhaps it's writing. Or drawing. Or cooking. Or singing, reading, painting, hiking, lifting weights, listening to sermons, or being in nature. How has God wired you to praise him outside of church? What horizontal activities can you turn vertical? Don't wait until Sunday morning to sip from the water fountain of praise. If you do, you'll show up to church as dry as a bone.

Loving Jesus More as We Tell Others about Him

The sixth and final water fountain is evangelism—sharing your faith with others. The passage says that "the Lord added to their number daily those who were being saved" (Acts 2 v 47). I'm assuming the early Christians were telling their friends about him.

Evangelism is the responsibility of every Christian. We're required to share our faith—whether we're comfortable doing so or not. Why? So people all over the world will know Christ. But evangelism isn't just for others. It changes *us*. We fall more in love with Jesus as we tell others about him.

How does this work? As we share our faith, we see God's Spirit in action. We see him perform miracles. We see the spiritually dead rise to life. We see addictions lose their power, sadness turn to joy, anxiety dissipate, broken relationships become reconciled, and fears vanish. We see guilt depart, shame dissolve, and sin die. We see people taste paradise for the first time. We see others fall in love with Jesus, and we fall more in love with him as they do.

Go tell others about Jesus. Share your faith. I dare you. Tell them what Christ has done in your life. Don't be bashful. Be bold. But also be ready. God might start performing miracles. He's got a habit of doing so.

Back to Ben and Carrie

What happened to Ben and Carrie? Did they make it as a couple?

They not only made it—they're thriving more than ever.

Ben finally spit out the saltwater of sex and started drinking living water. He began reading the Bible, spending time with other Christians, praying, giving away his time and money, praising God, and telling others about the miracle God had done in resurrecting his life. As he did, he was freed from the saltwater cycle that characterized the first decade of his marriage... freed from the toxic chains of sexual addiction... freed to love God, love his wife, and pursue both with an undivided heart. Carrie forgave him. They started drinking living water together. As they did, they fell more in love with each other. Their experience of vertical love for God overflowed into horizontal love for each other.

And they've never been better.

"We're on the brink of divorce and you're our last hope."

No way. I wasn't their last hope. Their last hope was Jesus. Their last hope was living water. And it did just the trick.

Will you join them for a drink?

6. QUENCHED

"We are not yet what we shall be, but we are growing toward it. The process is not yet finished, but it is going on. This is not the end, but it is the road. All does not yet gleam in glory, but all is being purified."

Martin Luther, *Defense of All the Articles*

My conversion story isn't sexy. It doesn't involve dreams, visions, healings, near-death experiences, exorcisms, crying statues, or liver shivers. I didn't weep. I didn't shake. I didn't speak in tongues. Nothing crazy happened. But that doesn't make the story less beautiful. Or less miraculous.

A Fresh Start

After my miserable freshman year at Michigan, I wanted a fresh start. So I transferred to the University of Illinois, where my identical twin brother, Bryan, was attending. Still sipping the saltwater of academics, I added a splash of another form—human approval. I joined Bryan's fraternity in search of the social affirmation that had eluded me at Michigan. The frat was filled with preppy prom kings, former jocks, and future investment bankers. Everybody was successful. Everybody was good-looking. Everybody had a gorgeous girlfriend. Everybody was attractive in every sense of the word. To this day I'm confused as to why they let me in.

The mission statement of the fraternity was simple—get your work done and party. As a blatant workaholic, the first half was music to my ears. The second half would require a lifestyle change. Somehow I'd have to add partying to my 16-hour daily study schedule. I wanted to be liked, so I made the proper adjustments. Drinking, smoking, bar-hopping, drugs, hook-ups, and all-night benders now supplemented my studies. I was a man of many hats. Well, two to be exact.

Was I happy? Nope. When I was partying, I felt guilty about not studying. When I was studying, I felt guilty about not partying. I was stressed, stretched, and sleep-deprived. My fraternity's mission statement wasn't working for me. I was physically exhausted. I was emotionally depleted. Something needed to change. ASAP.

Thankfully, God stepped in.

A Divine Intervention

One Friday night, I put on my party hat and went out drinking with my fraternity brothers. A close and concerned friend saw me drunk, lovingly pulled me aside, and bravely invited me to a weekly Christian gathering the following Wednesday night. I reluctantly accepted the invitation. After the meeting, I was excited. No, it wasn't the content of the meeting that excited me—it was the pretty girls. I came back week after week just to talk to them. You could say God used my hormones to expose me to Christianity.

After a few months, my attention shifted from the pretty girls to Jesus. I was intrigued by Christianity. Who was this man claiming to be God? What did these people mean by a "personal relationship" with him? Was I really sinful? Was I really loved by God? Was Christ the answer to my nagging internal emptiness? I began searching for answers. I met with Catholic priests, Protestant pastors, and campus ministers to investigate this curious religion. I attended church services across the entire campus. I annoyingly interviewed every Christian I knew.

Yet the penny wouldn't drop. Nobody could convince me that Christianity was true.

When did I first believe?

When I opened the Bible. Nine months after that first Christian gathering, I read from it for the first time. Once I started reading, I couldn't stop. I finished the New Testament in six months, after which I knew I had a decision to make. I could either reject Jesus as God and continue guzzling saltwater, or I could accept him as my personal Lord, Savior, and living-water source. I chose the latter. During my senior year of college, I drank living water for the first time. I became a Christian.

And all my problems were solved.

Yeah, right.

After becoming a Christian, did my vices vanish? Sort of. Did I spit out saltwater and saturate my heart with living water? Sort of. Did I experience the freedom, acceptance, security, peace, and love I was after? Sort of. Did I capture paradise lost? Sort of.

Was my thirst quenched? Sort of. Is it today? Sort of.

Sort of?

Yes. Sort of.

Theologians call this the "already but not yet" nature of the Christian life. We're already quenched. And yet we're *so* not yet quenched.

Already but Not Yet Quenched

When we believe in Jesus, he *does* promise to quench our thirst with his living water. He says to Insatia, "Whoever drinks the water I give them will *never thirst*" (John 4 v 14, italics added). Later in the same Gospel he says:

> I am the bread of life. Whoever comes to me will never go hungry, and whoever believes in me will *never be thirsty*. (John 6 v 35, italics added)

Jesus makes it clear that his living water can quench the thirst of *any* person who believes in him. Case closed. And yes, I've had moments when my thirst has felt quenched—when I've tasted paradise. All Christians are promised such tastes. For me, they typically happen when I'm drinking from one of the water fountains I described in chapter 5. For example, I'm listening to a song about Jesus and experience a sense of unmatchable joy. Or I'm praying after a stressful day and a feeling of inexplicable peace calms my soul. Or I'm writing this book and have a spiritual epiphany that excites and delights my heart.

I do get tastes of paradise. Not as frequently as I'd like, but they happen. I *already* experience the real-time, here-and-now, powerful presence of God's Spirit as I drink living water. I'm *already* filled with love, joy, peace, forbearance, kindness, goodness, faithfulness, gentleness, and self-control (Galatians 5 v 22-23). I'm *already* satisfied as God dwells within me. I'm *already* experiencing paradise lost.

I'm *already* quenched.

And yet, you'd only have to spend five minutes with me to realize I'm not yet fully quenched. I sin. I don't do what I should. I do what I shouldn't. I rarely experience the fruit of the Spirit at full strength. My thoughts wander to things I'm embarrassed to share. I profess faith in Christ but often live as if I'm not a Christian. In other words, I'm a hypocrite.

I'm already quenched, and yet I'm paradoxically not yet quenched.

The apostle Paul explains this "already but not yet" spiritual dynamic in his letter to the Galatians. He says this:

> For the flesh desires what is contrary to the Spirit,
> and the Spirit what is contrary to the flesh. They are
> in conflict with each other, so that you are not to do
> whatever you want. (Galatians 5 v 17)

Paul's point is that there are two competing forces in every Christian. The first is the Spirit of God. The second is our flesh—the part of us that wants nothing to do with God (see chapter 3, page 29). In our "already" moments, the Spirit is king and the flesh is dormant. We're deeply connected to God. We're displaying the fruit of the Spirit. We're one with Jesus. In our "not yet" moments, however, we feel enslaved to the flesh. It controls our hearts, minds, bodies, and souls—and it pushes us away from Christ. It leads us into sin.

We're Still Sipping

Why are our lives so riddled with these "not yet" moments? Because we're sipping living water. Emphasis on *sipping*. Instead of gulping it down as we should, we consume it in tiny amounts when we feel like it.

I'm a perfect example. Instead of meditating on Scripture day and night (Joshua 1 v 8), I read it in the morning and forget it by lunch. Instead of spending quality time with other Christians daily (Acts 2 v 42-46), I spend my free time reading, writing, and monitoring my favorite sports teams in isolation. Instead of praying continually (1 Thessalonians 5 v 17), I pray when I want something or when my life's in shambles. Instead of being rich in good deeds and generous with my money (1 Timothy 6 v 18), I cling to my time, energy, and income. Instead of constantly offering praise as a sacrifice to God (Hebrews 13 v 15), I frequently ignore him. Instead of loving God with my heart, soul, mind, and strength (Mark 12 v 30), I love him with only a teeny portion of me.

Because I so half-heartedly and infrequently sip living water, I'm not yet fully quenched.

Please Like Me!

Where does the "already but not yet" show up in my life? Everywhere. Take human approval as an example. As I mentioned, I was drinking the saltwater of human approval at Illinois, which led to the unsustainable work-party-work-party frat-life rhythm. Am I different now that I'm a Christian?

Sort of.

Yes, my longing to be popular has subsided. I'm content having fewer friendships. I'm fine being more socially isolated as I focus on my family, career, and God. I don't care if others think I'm cool. I risk rejection by sharing my faith boldly with people. I'm even okay if people don't like this book. Yes, I still love people and desire their love, but I don't *need* it. I'm daily spitting out the saltwater of human approval, drinking living water, and resting in God's approval of me.

And yet, in my flesh, I still *really* want to be popular.

An example? At the end of each month, I spend a Saturday morning balancing our family budget. The process causes me intense anxiety. Why? I sip saltwater while I do it. The form? Not money. Not security. Not possessions. Not anything obvious to the naked eye. I sip the saltwater of human approval—my wife's approval. Deep down, I want to earn Abby's love by earning money. If we're rich, she'll love me more. If we're poor, she'll love me less.

This is ridiculous, of course. Abby loves me for me—not my money. But my twisted mind has a way of deceiving itself when I'm knee-deep in financial spreadsheets. I convince myself that our wealth and her love will grow or shrink proportionally. I worship a wife who worships money—a wife who doesn't even exist. I want to be popular with one person— Abby—really, really badly. And so I worry as I balance our budget. Every month.

Already but not yet. I'm already free from the idol of human approval but not yet wholly free. I'm already spitting out saltwater and yet I'm still sipping it. I'm already drinking living water and yet I'm sometimes spitting it out. I'm already quenched but not yet fully quenched.

Fully Quenched in Heaven

Thankfully, the "already but not yet" isn't the end of the story. There *will* come a day when "already but not yet" will be shortened to "already." A day when I will be fully quenched. When *all* of Jesus' followers will be fully quenched. When the war between the Spirit and our flesh will be won by the Spirit. When paradise will be restored. The apostle John talks about this day in the book of Revelation. In chapter 7, he says this about God's people:

> "Never again will they hunger; never again will they thirst. The sun will not beat down on them," nor any scorching heat. For the Lamb at the center of the throne

will be their shepherd; "he will lead them to springs of living water."

"And God will wipe away every tear from their eyes." (Revelation 7 v 16-17)

In chapter 21, John goes into much greater detail of how this will happen:

Then I saw a "new heaven and a new earth," for the first heaven and the first earth had passed away, and there was no longer any sea. I saw the Holy City, the new Jerusalem, coming down out of heaven from God, prepared as a bride beautifully dressed for her husband. And I heard a loud voice from the throne saying, "Look! God's dwelling place is now among the people, and he will dwell with them. They will be his people, and God himself will be with them and be their God. 'He will wipe every tear from their eyes. There will be no more death' or mourning or crying or pain, for the old order of things has passed away."

He who was seated on the throne said, "I am making everything new!" Then he said, "Write this down, for these words are trustworthy and true." (Revelation 21 v 1-5)

What will the eternal "already" look like? First, it will look nothing like this world. Everything will be made new. *Everything.* The physical world around us will be new. Our bodies will be new. Our relationships will be new. Our minds will be new. Our hearts will be new. Everything and everybody will be made new. Brand. Spankin'. New.

Second, the "heat"—the suffering—of this life will disappear. This broken world will be broken no more.

There will be no more grieving or worrying. No more anger, aggravation, insecurity, irritation, hatred, or heartache. No more violence or crime. No more money troubles. No more breakups. No more stresses, strains, aches, or pains. No more suffering at all. The heat will vanish. Completely.

Third, God will live with us permanently. This means no more intermittent trips to water fountains—we'll be hooked up to living water IVs. Jesus will be our perfect Shepherd. We'll worship him perfectly. We'll experience the paradise that humanity had to leave in the Garden of Eden. We'll dwell in a new garden. A new heaven. A new earth. A world of perfection. Our thirst will be finally quenched. Forever.

Forever.

Join Me

I had a choice to make during my senior year of college. I could either pour out my saltwater or keep refilling my glass. I could either confess my sinfulness or turn a blind eye to it. I could either quench my thirst with living water or keep sipping saltwater.

I chose living water.

God is inviting you to choose the same drink. Perhaps for the first time. He's inviting you to place your faith in Jesus as your Lord and Savior. He's inviting you to pour out your saltwater and drink the beverage that will never leave you thirsty again.

If you're ready to accept his invitation, I'd encourage you to do three things. First, let him know. Turn to him in prayer and tell him you're ready to pour out your saltwater and drink his living water. Tell him you're ready to surrender your life to him as your God. Tell him you're ready to drink the water that will well up to eternal life (John 4 v 14).

Second, talk to a mature Christian about your decision—somebody who can guide you as you begin your Christian journey. Talk to a pastor. Talk to a trusted Christian friend. Talk to anybody with a strong Christian faith. Don't begin this wonderful new life alone.

Third, link arms with me. Join me in battle as our flesh and the Spirit duke it out. We'll be already quenched but not yet quenched. It will be beautiful and ugly. Effortless and exhausting. Up and down. Back and forth. It will be a fight. Well, more like a war.

But one day the war will end. The Spirit will win. Evil will fall to the wayside. Jesus will prevail. And we will be with him in paradise for eternity.

I hope to see you there.

7. GOD-GARBAGE-GIFT

"For everything God created is good, and nothing is to be
rejected if it is received with thanksgiving."

1 Timothy 4 v 4

This brief chapter explains the structure of the next eight. The format is simple: *god-garbage-gift*. These are three ways we commonly treat any form of saltwater. We can swing the pendulum in one direction and idolize it, turning it into a **god**. We can swing the pendulum to the opposite extreme and demonize it, turning it into **garbage**. Or we can use it as God intended and treat it as a **gift** from above.

In all three instances, we're putting our hope in something. In the first, we're putting our hope in the saltwater itself. In the second, we're putting our hope in avoiding the saltwater. In the third, our hope is in the giver of the saltwater—Jesus Christ.

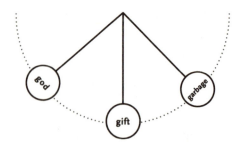

As an illustration, let's look at the saltwater of caffeine.

Candice is a coffee addict. She's harsh toward her family before her morning cup. She stops into Starbucks three times a day and orders a venti americano with five shots of espresso. *Five shots.* Her monthly coffee budget triples her car payment. She can't function without caffeine. It's her god.

Stephanie avoids caffeine at all costs. She believes it makes her body tainted in God's eyes. While she admits this self-imposed prohibition may seem excessive to others, she believes there's a special blessing awaiting her in heaven if she abstains. So she self-righteously restricts herself, and looks down on anyone who does otherwise. She's turned caffeine into garbage. In doing so, she's worshiping the false god of a chemical-free body.

Mary's a Christian. During the week she limits herself to two daily cups of coffee—one before work and one after lunch. On Saturday morning she adds a bonus drink. She treats herself to a 7-11 Big Gulp—a mix of fountain Cherry Coke and Diet Coke. 32 ounces of carbonated and caffeinated glory. As soon as the elongated red plastic straw hits her lips, she smiles cheek to cheek with a gleeful chuckle and a "Thank you, Jesus!" Within an hour, the soda's gone. And her day continues. To Mary, caffeine's a gift from God. Nothing more. Nothing less.

Three women. Three different responses to caffeine. Candice treats it as a god. Stephanie treats it as garbage. Mary treats it as a gift from God.

Each of the following eight chapters will follow this same format: god-garbage-gift. I'll tackle eight forms of saltwater to show how we can treat each as a god, demonize each as garbage, or worship God for giving each as a gift. This list certainly isn't exhaustive, but it's a good start. And they're in no particular order, so you can read them in whatever sequence you prefer, or just choose those that strike you as most relevant.

God-garbage-gift. How do *you* treat saltwater?

8. MONEY

"Money never made a man happy yet, nor will it …
The more a man has, the more he wants. Instead of its
filling a vacuum, it makes one."

Benjamin Franklin

Payday.

The word is music to most people's ears. It's a day to watch your bank balance rise. A day to pay off your bills and credit cards. A day to splurge on golf clubs, shoes, or a night on the town. It's a day that keeps people going.

While I was a pastor in Manhattan, however, I dreaded it. I was anxious for days leading up to it. Payday—a once-a-month event—put a pit in my stomach. Why?

I never knew how much I'd make. 100% of my paycheck came from a set of remarkably generous yet *highly* unpredictable monthly donors. Sometimes they'd forget to donate. Sometimes they'd quit giving without telling me. Sometimes they'd give less than they'd promised. Sometimes they'd give *more* than they'd promised. One thing was certain—payday was a guessing game. And not a fun one.

But what was at the *root* of my anxiety in the days leading up to payday? Was it just the unknown of my paycheck amount?

No. I was sipping saltwater—the saltwater of money. Instead of trusting in God, I was allowing my income (or lack thereof) to rule my heart, mind, and emotions. Instead of believing God would supply all my needs (Matthew 6 v 31-33), I was ignoring him and fearing I'd go broke. Instead of putting my hope in Christ, I was putting it in a dollar amount. Instead of drinking living water, I was drinking the saltwater of money.

You might be too.

GOD: Salvation by Accumulation

The subject of money was important to Jesus. So important that he talked about it more than about heaven and hell combined. So important that eleven of his parables mention it. So important that only one subject—the kingdom of God—receives more attention in the Gospels.

The Rich Young Man

In one money-related passage, Jesus has a conversation with a young tycoon clearly guzzling the saltwater of money. Here's a clip of the story from the Gospel of Matthew:

> Just then a man came up to Jesus and asked, "Teacher, what good thing must I do to get eternal life?"
>
> "Why do you ask me about what is good?" Jesus replied. "There is only One who is good. If you want to enter life, keep the commandments."
>
> "Which ones?" he inquired.

Jesus replied, "'You shall not murder, you shall not commit adultery, you shall not steal, you shall not give false testimony, honor your father and mother,' and 'love your neighbor as yourself.'"

"All these I have kept," the young man said. "What do I still lack?"

Jesus answered, "If you want to be perfect, go, sell your possessions and give to the poor, and you will have treasure in heaven. Then come, follow me."

When the young man heard this, he went away sad, because he had great wealth. (Matthew 19 v 16-22)

All this man had to do to gain eternal life was to let go of his fortune and follow Jesus. That's it. And he would get a huge payoff. Not only would he get into heaven, but he would get *treasure* in heaven (v 21). But he couldn't do it. He couldn't surrender the dough. He couldn't pour out his saltwater.

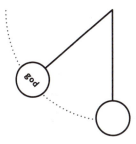

The lesson here? If you're wealthy, beware. Money is a tasty form of saltwater. So tasty that this man turned down heaven to keep his fortune. So tasty that it can lure faithful Christians away from Christ (1 Timothy 6 v 10). So tasty that Jesus says it's easier for a camel to go through the eye of a needle than for a rich person to enter the kingdom of God (Matthew 19 v 24). In other words, it's tough to be loaded and follow Christ. So tough that Jesus says it would be impossible, but for the work of God in us (Matthew 19 v 25-26).

Poor Slaves

But what if you're *not* wealthy like the rich young man? What if you're poor? Can you still be sipping the saltwater of money? Do you need to *have* money to be drinking the saltwater of money?

You don't. A person with very little money can worship it as fervently as a tight-fisted billionaire. Consider two examples.

Scott's a low-paid minister obsessively committed to pinching pennies in the name of "good stewardship." He forces his stay-at-home wife, Laura, to spend hours a day clipping coupons, and berates her when she forgets to use one. He spends his afternoons in coffee shops but brings his own coffee from home. Although his family is exhausted and desperate for a vacation (they haven't taken one in ten years), he refuses to travel because he sees it as a frivolous expense. He begrudgingly buys his kids new clothes and only if the old ones have holes in them. He won't replace his wife's dangerously old car. His house is falling apart but he won't spend a dime fixing it. He begins and ends his days worrying about money and has been doing so for 20 years.

Joyce is a recent college grad and an entry-level social worker making a tiny salary. As a Christian, she's been taught to give a portion of her wages to the church, but she won't do so until her college loans are paid off—in ten years. Although she can afford her monthly rent, she lies about her income to her parents and they cover it. She purchases clothes, leaves the tags on, wears them three or four times, and returns them. She intentionally "forgets" her wallet when dining out with friends and tips at 8% when she does pay. She steals office supplies from work and cheats on her taxes. She constantly checks her bank balance and has panic attacks when it dips. She can't stop thinking about money.

Scott and Joyce have two things in common. Both are relatively poor—at least according to privileged Western standards. Both, however, are slaves to the god of money. They love it with the same fervor as the rich young man.

GARBAGE: Salvation by Poverty

Many of us worship money. But some people swing the pendulum in the other direction and demonize it—viewing it as "garbage." They take pride in their poverty. They look down on the wealthy. They take drastic measures to avoid high salaries, comfortable lifestyles, and worldly luxuries. To these people, money is evil.

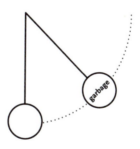

Not surprisingly, the majority of those who demonize money do so in the name of religion. Consider the Christian monastic movement. Launched in the late third century and still present today, its goal is to isolate Christians from the outside world, eliminate unnecessary temptations, and provide a distractionless setting to commune with God. A vow of poverty is common. The implicit message in such a vow, of course, is that money is an obstacle to God. It seduces us into self-indulgence. It clouds our vision of the Divine. It's a weapon of Satan and an enemy to holiness. The godliest people avoid it.

But there's a major problem with the monastic take on money. By demonizing it, monks and nuns are creating an alternative idol. They're worshiping the god of need. They're making self-deprivation something it was never meant to be—a pathway to piety. They're equating poverty with holiness and ignoring the fact that many of the holiest heroes of the Bible—Abraham, Joseph, and David to name a few—were quite wealthy. In the end, they're villainizing money and exalting the absence of it. In doing so, they're ironically taking their eyes off the God they claim to be drastically searching for and placing them on an alternative savior.

But I Don't Live in a Monastery

Okay, you're not a monk or a nun. Can you still be demonizing money—specifically in the name of religion and even more specifically in the name of Christianity? Of course. Take Beth as an example.

Beth's a middle-aged, middle-class housewife with three kids and a husband who works in construction. She drives a used minivan and lives in an old three-bedroom ranch. She attends a large evangelical megachurch and is very much devoted to God. She reads her Bible every day, prays diligently, and serves at a homeless shelter on Friday nights. Her friends admire her. Her pastor adores her. On the outside, she looks squeaky clean.

The problem? Every Sunday, she falls into the same pattern. She sees Christians pulling up to church in fancy cars, wearing fancy clothes, and driving home to fancy houses—and she condemns them. To Beth, their money is a sign of spiritual immaturity. She believes they're all caught up in lives of materialism and greed and are certainly less "Christian" than her. She smiles at them when they walk by at church but chastises them in her heart. Although she'll never admit it, they're her enemies. And in her mind, they're God's enemies too.

The sin in Beth's heart? Judgmentalism. She's angry, critical, and self-righteous. She's sipping the saltwater of poverty. She has demonized money and anybody in possession of it.

GIFT: The Gift of Money

In the end, when we idolize money, we exalt being rich. When we demonize money, we exalt being poor. How can we do neither? How should we approach money?

The Parable of the Talents

In Matthew 25 v 14-30, Jesus shares what is commonly referred to as the parable of the talents—a talent in those days being a unit of money worth roughly twenty years' salary for a day laborer. To summarize the story, a master is going away on a journey and entrusts three servants with his wealth. To the first servant he gives five talents, to the second two, and to the third one. The servant with five talents uses his wealth to produce five more talents—a 100% profit. The second servant also does well and multiplies his two talents into four. The third servant, however, digs a hole in the ground and buries his one talent.

When the master returns, he's pleased with the first two men and says to both:

> Well done, good and faithful servant! You have been faithful with a few things; I will put you in charge of many things. Come and share your master's happiness! (Matthew 25 v 21, 23)

The master isn't so happy with the third servant. He refers to him as "wicked" and "lazy" (v 26), not to mention idiotic for failing to gain interest on his talent at a local bank. In fact, he's so infuriated that he makes the third servant give his only talent to the man with ten, and sends him into the darkness "where there will be weeping and gnashing of teeth" (v 30).

Ouch.

Three quick takeaways on how to view money from this story:

On Loan

First, we don't own it. God does. We're merely borrowing it. *All* our money is on temporary loan from God. Just like the three servants' talents. This means we should be ready and willing to give it back to him should he tell us to do so. Our grip on it must be loose, our affections toward it must be light, and the chains that bind our hearts to it must be cut. Also, if you're rich, don't be proud of it. You're only rich because God has given you a bigger loan. And on the flipside, if you aren't rich, don't be ashamed of it, for God has—in his wisdom and goodness—lovingly chosen to loan you less. Put simply, your net worth and your self-worth aren't the same thing.

Go Make Money

Second, God isn't opposed to us making money. In fact, he loves when we do so. He wants us to work hard and multiply the wealth he loans us. That's why the master is so pleased with the first two servants. And as the rest of the Bible shows us, there's a reason why he wants us to make more money. He wants us to bless others. He wants us to be hospitable, generous, charitable, unselfish, and liberal with our giving. He wants us to wisely provide for loved ones, strangers, and anybody in need. He wants us to feed the hungry, clothe the naked, and house the homeless (e.g. Proverbs 22 v 9; 28 v 27; Matthew 25 v 31-46). God isn't against us spending money on ourselves, but his vision extends far beyond this. He wants us to help others with our money.

A Big Deal

Third, money's a big deal to God. The fate of the one-talent servant makes this clear. Why such a big deal? Because our posture toward money is a great litmus test of our posture toward God. If we love money, we'll hate God. If we love God, we won't love money. Simple as that. Jesus makes this clear in his Sermon on the Mount (Matthew 5, 6 and 7):

> No one can serve two masters. Either you will hate the one and love the other, or you will be devoted to the one and despise the other. You cannot serve both God and money. (Matthew 6 v 24)

Can't Just Pour It Out

To close the chapter, let's go all the way back to Sam Polk from chapter three. To his credit, he admitted he was a money addict. He even took steps to pour out his saltwater. Once he realized his addiction, he quit his job on Wall Street. He started visiting jails to speak with inmates about *their* unique money addictions. He launched a nonprofit business to help low-income families. He even publicly challenged his former Wall Street colleagues to give 25% of their annual bonuses to those living in poverty.

But did he ever kick his money addiction? Did he ever become fully free? Did the toxic chains ever fall completely off? Nope. At the end of the article, he admits his money addiction still haunts him. He cites his habit of buying lottery tickets as evidence.

Why can't Polk seem to kick his insatiable thirst for money? One reason. To my knowledge, although he's poured out his saltwater, he hasn't replaced it with living water. He hasn't consumed the drink that tastes better than ten trillion dollars. He hasn't satisfied himself with Christ. Until he does, he'll keep sipping saltwater.

If you're drinking the saltwater of money, first pour it out. Give generously. Live modestly. Care for the poor. Stop accumulating for the sake of accumulating. Stop seeking salvation in your salary. Stop storing up treasures on earth. But don't stop there. Start following Jesus. Start drinking living water. Start worshiping Christ. Start seeking salvation in the only Savior who will satisfy your soul in a way money never could.

Then you will have treasure in heaven.

9. SEX

Guess how many sex addicts live in America.

50,000?

Higher.

100,000?

Higher.

500,000?

Still too low.

According to a 2014 article posted by the American Association for Marriage and Family Therapy, nearly *12 million* people in the United States are sex addicts—people who compulsively participate in sexual activity despite life-damaging consequences. That's more than the populations of Wyoming, Vermont, North Dakota, Alaska, South Dakota, Delaware, Montana, Rhode Island, New Hampshire, Maine, and Hawaii *combined*. And I presume the estimate's on the low end, as sex addicts rarely admit to being sex addicts.

Why has sexual addiction become such an epidemic? Some people blame the internet for making sexual experimentation more available and anonymous than ever. Others blame television for its rampant glamorization of sexual expression and sexual freedom. Some even blame our phones for making "sexting" and mobile pornography common practice. But what's the *real* cause of sexual addiction? Can we blame technology?

No way. A person becomes a sex addict for one reason. Sex is saltwater—perhaps in its most seductive form. And a sex addict becomes a sex addict by sipping it.

GOD: Salvation by Porn

Let me explain a calculated vocabulary choice. I'm using a well-known word with a strong cultural connotation to describe all versions of sex-flavored saltwater consumption:

Porn.

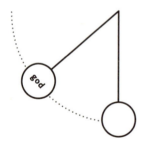

But porn here isn't short for pornography. It's short for *porneia*—a Greek word that appears 26 times in the New Testament. *Porneia* is used to describe *any* type of sexual immorality—premarital sex, homosexuality, extramarital affairs, prostitution, rape... *anything* of a deviant sexual nature. Porneia—or porn for short—is any form of sex outside a heterosexual marriage bed.

I'm going to divide porn into two categories: *virtual* porn and *live* porn. Virtual porn is precisely what it sounds like—

fake sex. It usually involves sexually pleasuring oneself to erotic videos, photos, conversations, stories, or mental images. Live porn, on the other hand, happens in real life in real time with real people.

Let me introduce you to a biblical hero who famously indulged in live porn.

King David

In 2 Samuel 11 we find the true tale of David and Bathsheba. The story takes place in the spring—the time of year when kings went off to war. For some reason, this spring King David is home on vacation. One night, he can't sleep. He gets out of bed and takes a stroll around his palace roof. Here's what happens:

> From the roof he saw a woman bathing. The woman was very beautiful, and David sent someone to find out about her. The man said, "She is Bathsheba, the daughter of Eliam and the wife of Uriah the Hittite." Then David sent messengers to get her. She came to him, and he slept with her. (2 Samuel 11 v 2-4)

After seeing Bathsheba naked, David treats himself to a little live porn.

What happens next?

> Then she went back home. The woman conceived and sent word to David, saying, "I am pregnant." (v 4-5)

He's knocked her up. Rats.

His next move? In a state of panic, David attempts a cover-up. He calls for Bathsheba's husband, Uriah—a soldier in David's army—and sends him home. Why? So he'll have sex with Bathsheba, the world will think the baby is Uriah's, and David will be off the hook (remember, they didn't have paternity tests back then). Uriah's response to David?

> The ark and Israel and Judah are staying in tents, and my commander Joab and my lord's men are camped in the open country. How could I go to my house to eat and drink and make love to my wife? As surely as you live, I will not do such a thing! (v 11)

David even tries to get him drunk so he'll go home. But Uriah won't take the bait. He's too loyal a soldier to do so.

So David comes up with a backup plan. He'll have Uriah killed in battle. At least then the solider won't be alive to deny the baby's his. How does David make sure he's killed? He tells Joab to put Uriah on the front line where the fighting's fiercest and to withdraw without him. Joab follows David's orders and Uriah dies. More accurately, David murders him.

What started with porn ends with cold-blooded killing.

While many lessons can be taken from this story, I'd like to highlight two—both revolving around porn.

Porn Will Change You

First, if you sip the saltwater of sex like David—if you partake in porn—it will change you. It will corrupt your heart, twist your values, and turn you into an animal. Look at David. This was "a man after [God's] own heart" (Acts 13 v 22). This was the anointed leader of God's chosen people (1 Samuel 16). This was an ancestor of Jesus himself (Matthew 1). And after one porn binge, he turns into a bloodthirsty savage. He forgets who he is. He forgets what he stands for. He forgets about God. He becomes unrecognizable.

How will porn change *you*? No, it probably won't turn you into a murderer like David, but it *will* mess with your head.

Take Tom as an example. He's been married to Bonnie just six months. Prior to their wedding day, he'd been knee-deep in virtual and live porn for fourteen years. He hung out in strip clubs, visited prostitutes, watched sex tapes, hooked up at bars... you name it. As a result, he now has what I call "porn brain damage." It shows itself in three ways.

First, his mind's been programmed to view women through one lens—a sexual lens. When he sees a female, he automatically undresses her with his eyes and imagines having sex with her. It's as instinctive as breathing. He knows it's wrong, but he can't stop it.

Second, porn's become the *only* way his brain and body can become sexually aroused. He needs the novelty, deception, and risk that go with it to be stimulated. Since none of these are present in bed with Bonnie, he's physically unable to have sex with her. Think erectile dysfunction.

Third, he has an endless mental rolodex of sexual images burnt into his memory. They haunt him. They tempt him. They lure him into feelings of resentment toward Bonnie for failing to measure up. They make him regret getting married. And Bonnie knows it.

No, Tom's not a murderer. He's a horny, spiteful, and tormented man. Porn's messed with his head. It's darkened his heart toward his wife. It's put a chasm between him and God. It's made him miserable.

And it will do the same to you.

Porn Will Hurt People
Lesson two from the story of David and Bathsheba is this: porn doesn't only hurt the perpetrator; it hurts *others*. It crushes spouses. It puts distance between loved ones. Worst of all, it slaps God in the face. Hard.

Back to David. How does his one act of porn affect others? To start with, Bathsheba gets pregnant and Uriah dies. But one chapter later we see three more consequences from the hand of God: The nation of Israel is given a war sentence for the rest of David's life, David's wives are given to other men who publicly rape them, and David's child with Bathsheba dies (2 Samuel 12 v 10-14). Ouch. *Many* people—not just David—are hurt by his porn.

How will porn hurt others in your life? People might not get pregnant, die, or be sent off to war, but people *will* suffer. Let's look at Tom again. First, he's made Bonnie deeply insecure, sexually frustrated, and confused. She never thought she'd be married to a porn addict, and she wants out. Then there are the women he ogles each day. He makes them feel objectified, dehumanized, and disgusted. Finally, there are the strangers he's unknowingly hurt for over a decade. He's had sex with women he didn't know were forced into prostitution, watched pornography of sexually-trafficked girls, and contributed thousands of dollars to nightclubs run by men committed to abusing and degrading females. Yes, Tom's porn is destroying him. But it's hurting others far worse.

And so will yours.

GARBAGE: Salvation by Abstinence

Not everybody worships sex like King David or Tom. In fact some people—although it's *very* rare in today's culture—demonize sex. And like those who demonize money, most of these people do it for religious reasons. Take Alley as an example.

Alley was raised in a non-religious family. In high school, her close friend invited her to a church youth group. Alley loved it. At the very first meeting she became a Christian.

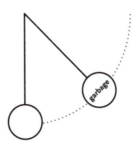

During college, she felt called to become a missionary. She was particularly enamored with and inspired by the life of the apostle Paul—by his courage, boldness, and willingness to abstain from worldly pleasures for the sake of telling people about Jesus. She wanted to be *just* like him.

After college, Alley immediately hit the mission field. Her first stop was an isolated village in North Africa. The first year went relatively smoothly. She learned the local language quickly, enthusiastically studied African culture, and filled her time with exciting new adventures. Life on the mission field was wonderful.

But things got hard during her second year. She contracted malaria. She was robbed. She broke her arm in a biking accident. But the worst part was the isolation. She was lonely. The only way she knew to cope was to remember the apostle Paul's life of sacrifice, and to focus on Jesus' words in Matthew 16:

> Then Jesus said to his disciples, "Whoever wants to be my disciple **must deny themselves** and take up their cross and follow me." (Matthew 16 v 24, bold text mine)

Alley is now in her third year as a missionary, and things have only gotten worse. She's sick all the time. She's tired and weary at the minimal success she's having in converting Africans to Christianity. She's lonelier than ever. She lacks joy.

She's forgotten the reasons why she entered the mission field in the first place. She's physically, emotionally, and spiritually miserable.

In her weakened state, she's also fallen into a sinful pattern. She judges her Christian friends back home for their "easy lives." She belittles them in her heart for getting married, having sex, making babies, and conforming to social norms. She looks down on them for their refusal to *seriously* obey Matthew 16 v 24 and deny themselves as she does. In her worst moments, she even questions their salvation. She wears a figurative badge of honor for her celibacy, and condemns those unwilling to wear the same badge.

Alley is doing two things. She's demonizing sex, marriage, and family. And she's idolizing abstinence, sacrifice, and self-denial.

Sadly, she no longer resembles the apostle Paul.

GIFT: The Gift of Sex

Millions of people around the world are idolizing sex—turning it into a god. Alley and a smaller subset of people are demonizing it—turning it into garbage. Both approaches are skewed and unhealthy. How, then, are we supposed to treat sex? How should we approach this touchy (no pun intended) subject?

The Bad News

Before I go any further, I need to make a concession: porn offers many things that you'll miss if you abstain from it. It offers novelty—new partners, poses, pictures, and plots—with each adventure. It offers variety—blonds, brunettes, men, women, and people of every kind—whatever or whomever you want, usually whenever you want it. It offers adrenaline—a rush as you enter into risky and secretive situations. It offers freedom—the ability to leave your partner at the drop of a hat. Ultimately, for a short amount of time, it can make you feel like a god.

Yes, if you abstain from porn, you'll miss out on this. That's the bad news.

The Good News

The good news, however, is that if you limit sex to the marriage bed, you'll get far more than you could ever get with porn. You might not have a novel sexual encounter every time you make love to your spouse, but you'll have deep comfort in the familiarity and lasting security that marital sex offers. You might not have access to multiple partners in a variety of shapes and sizes, but you'll have unwavering access to one partner who truly knows you, accepts you, and loves you for who you are. You might not experience the adrenaline rush that comes with porn, but you'll have a guilt-free, shame-free, and fear-free sense of peace before, during, and after sex. You might not have the freedom to leave your spouse after sex, but you'll have the safety of knowing that your spouse will also never leave you. You might not feel like a god, but you'll experience God's love as you love and honor your spouse during sex. That's the good news.

What If You're Single?

But what if—like Alley—you're a single Christian committed to celibacy? Is there still good news? Yes. The good news is that the single, celibate life—if done right—can be even richer than the married, sex-filled life. Why? A single person has more time and freedom to invest in Christ (1 Corinthians 7 v 7-8, 32-34). And Christ is better than sex. Far better.

Sex offers pleasure, but Christ offers soul-penetrating joy. Sex offers intimacy with a romantic partner, but Christ offers spiritual union with the God of the universe. Sex offers stress relief, but Christ offers peace that transcends understanding. Sex is beautiful, but Christ is infinitely more beautiful. You've heard the phrase "(blank) is better than sex"? Well, Christ is better than sex. And being single means you'll have more time for him.

More Good News

But there's even better news. And it applies to *all* of us—married or single.

Your tainted sexual history does not define you.

If you've sipped the saltwater of sex—and we all have—there's hope. Christ offers forgiveness for all your sexual failures. All your one-night stands. All your porn binges. Every sexual sin you've ever committed. *Forgiven.* No guilt. No shame. No condemnation. He wipes away your sexual failures; he discards them as far as the east is from the west (Psalm 103 v 12).

But there are two conditions. First, you must confess your sexual sin to God. 1 John 1 says this:

> If we claim to be without sin, we deceive ourselves and
> the truth is not in us. If we confess our sins, he is faithful
> and just and will forgive us our sins and purify us from
> all unrighteousness. (1 John 1 v 8-9)

Second, you must commit to change. Colossians 3 says this:

> Put to death, therefore, whatever belongs to your earthly
> nature: sexual immorality [*porneia*], impurity, lust, evil
> desires and greed, which is idolatry. (Colossians 3 v 5)

We must put our sexual sin to death. We must violently fight against sexual temptation using the Spirit of God, the Bible, and fellow Christians as our weapons. We must replace our affections for porn with affections for Jesus.

Does this sound too hard? Or unrealistic, knowing how often and easily *porneia* pops into your mind? Then grab hold of this promise from God:

> No temptation has overtaken you except what is
> common to mankind. And God is faithful; he will not let
> you be tempted beyond what you can bear. But when you
> are tempted, he will also provide a way out so that you
> can endure it. (1 Corinthians 10 v 13)

We must spit out the saltwater of sex and drink living water. And God promises to help us do it.

Will you?

10. CONTROL

Trump Triumphs.

This was the *New York Times* website headline the morning I wrote this chapter. Donald Trump had just been elected as the 45th President of the United States. The news was stunning. It sent shock waves across the country and the world. It certainly sent shock waves across my twin brother Bryan's apartment.

I spoke with Bryan—a financial advisor for a reputable investment firm—that Wednesday morning. His response to the news? *Panic.* Why? Not because he was concerned about politics. He was panicking for one reason—a business reason.

He was afraid he'd lose clients.

His logic? Trump, like any new president, meant uncertainty for America. Uncertainty for America would cause the stock market to crash. If the stock market crashed, his clients would lose money and blame Bryan. If they lost enough, they'd dump Bryan and find a new financial advisor.

But what was at the core of Bryan's panic that morning? He was panicking because his life felt out of control. He couldn't control the future. He couldn't control the markets. He couldn't control his clients' reactions to the markets. He couldn't control if they stayed or jumped ship. He couldn't control *anything*. And it led him to panic.

Put another way, Bryan was sipping saltwater that morning—the saltwater of control. And if you've ever worried like Bryan—about *anything*—you've sipped the same drink. I sip it all the time.

GOD: Salvation by Kung Fu Grip

It's tricky to identify when we're sipping the saltwater of control. As with Bryan, a more obvious idol—in his case his business—is often hiding the deeper core idol of control.

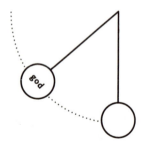

Let me give a few examples. Bill struggles with OCD and spends six hours a day—*every* day—cleaning his studio apartment. His obvious idol, cleanliness, is hiding his core idol—control over his living space. Susan spends every ounce of her free time obsessively scrolling through dating websites looking for her future husband. Her obvious idol, marriage, is hiding her core idol—control over her future. Josh works out three hours a day, seven days a week, and gets anxious if he can't get to the gym. His obvious idol, fitness, is hiding his core idol—control over his body.

Control worshipers are often worshiping an obvious god other than control. But if you dig deep enough, control is at the heart of their idolatry.

Let's look at a woman whose obvious idol, *motherhood*, was hiding her core idol—control over how and when it would happen.

Sarah

In Genesis 11, we're introduced to Sarai, whose name is later changed to Sarah. She's married to Abram, later called Abraham. In Genesis 12, God says this to Abraham:

> Go from your country, your people and your father's
> household to the land I will show you. I will make you
> into a great nation, and I will bless you; I will make your
> name great, and you will be a blessing. I will bless those
> who bless you, and whoever curses you I will curse;
> and all peoples on earth will be blessed through you.
> (Genesis 12 v 1-3)

In other words, God's got a big plan for Abraham. The entire world will be blessed through him. The necessary ingredient to this plan is descendants. Abraham and Sarah must have descendants. Lots and lots of descendants. At this time they have none, but God makes it clear they've got nothing to worry about. In the next chapter he tells Abraham:

> I will make your offspring like the dust of the earth, so
> that if anyone could count the dust, then your offspring
> could be counted. (Genesis 13 v 16)

The only problem is that God never tells Abraham when this will take place. By the time chapter 16 rolls around, he's 85-ish, Sarah's 75-ish, and they're still childless.

So Sarah takes matters into her own hands. She takes a sip of saltwater, tells Abraham to sleep with her servant Hagar, and tries to build a family through her (apparently this was socially acceptable back then). Abraham concedes and they have sex. Hagar gets pregnant and Sarah gets her wish— she can start a family by counting Hagar's baby as her own. Problem solved.

Yeah, right.

As usual, a sip of saltwater results in nothing but trouble for the sipper.

The Hangover

After sipping the saltwater of control, Sarah suffers a painful hangover symptom—a series of fractured relationships.

First, Hagar becomes her enemy. As soon as Hagar conceives, she becomes bitter at Sarah (v 4). I suspect I'd feel the same way if I was forced to have a baby and hand it over to my boss for life.

Second, Sarah and Abraham get into a fight (v 5). She has the gall to blame *him* for Hagar's bitterness, as if the adulterous exchange was his idea. Abraham casually dismisses Sarah's blame-shifting attempt and tells her to handle Hagar herself. So she does. By abusing her.

Finally, there's the unspoken division between Sarah and God. She's worshiping a false god, making it impossible to worship the true God. That's just how idolatry works. Saltwater and living water don't mix well together.

How does God handle things? How does he respond to Sarah's idolatry? Does he punish her?

Nope. He shows her grace. He promises she'll *still* have a son of her own (Genesis 17 v 16). He delivers on this promise in chapter 21 when she gives birth to Isaac. *At 90 years old.*

God still carries out his promises to Abraham. And he still uses Sarah to do it. But he does it in his way and in his timing.

The Lesson

> Many are the plans in a person's heart, but it is the LORD's purpose that prevails. (Proverbs 19 v 21)

Sarah thought her plan would work. She thought she could make a baby on her own terms and everything would turn out okay. She thought she could rip control right out of God's hands and place it in her own. But no matter how much saltwater she drank, God's plan still prevailed. He did what he was going to do when he was going do it. He was in charge—not her.

The same goes for us. We may *think* we're in control. We may *think* we can dictate our destinies. We may *think* we can micromanage our futures and steal control from God. But we can't. He's managing everything.

So let go. Spit out the saltwater of control. There's really no point in drinking it.

GARBAGE: Salvation by Chaos

What might it look like to demonize control? To swing the pendulum in the opposite direction and worship the god of chaos?

Let's look at Sean.

Sean

I met Sean—a recovering cocaine addict—at the Boston Rescue Mission. He was a high-strung, middle-aged resident in the mission's long-term recovery program. When I was introduced to Sean, he'd been living there only a few weeks.

We bonded quickly. He attended my weekly Bible studies. He picked my brain about Christianity. He came to me for professional and personal advice. If Sean had a question, I was his man. We became close friends fast.

For two months, Sean did quite well at the mission. He never missed a chore. He made it to group therapy every afternoon. He attended chapel every evening. He was drug-free for 60 days for the first time in five years. Sean's life was turning around.

And then one night he took a two-hour pass and didn't come back.

The mission staff team was perplexed. Of all the residents, Sean's trajectory seemed to be the most promising. Many even predicted he'd be on staff at the mission after he graduated from the program. Why would he throw it all away? Why would he return to the streets? Why would he go back to the destructive, dead-end lifestyle of a drug addict?

I found out a month later when Sean returned to the mission to give recovery another try. He came straight to me and shared his reason for leaving. "Steve," he said, "You've gotta know something about me. I'm a screw-up. That's just who I am. I was a screw-up in high school, a screw-up in college, and now I'm a screw-up as an adult. I'm used to things being out of control and, well, (expletive)'d up. I'm used to drama. I'm used to getting into fights. I'm used to being addicted to coke. I'm used to having *no* control over my life. It's the only world I know. And as messed up as it sounds, I'm comfortable in it. So when I came to the mission and started getting my life in order, it made me uneasy. I wasn't used to the success, the progress, the praise... any of it. I felt like I was in a foreign country and I wasn't supposed to be there. So I bolted."

To Sean, the mission represented predictability, security, order, and safety. It represented control. One might assume this to be a good thing. Not for Sean. He wanted chaos. And he found it as a drug addict. The irony? By seeking out chaos, he was actually controlling his world. He was just making sure it was out of control.

What happened to Sean? In his second go-around, he made it even further through the program. He got clean. He got healthy. He made it through 11 of the program's 12 steps. And then he panicked again. And he bolted back to the streets.

This time, he never returned.

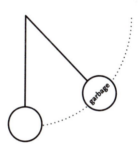

And you?

What about *you*? How do you worship the god of chaos? For each of us it can look quite different. Perhaps you're involved in an unhealthy romantic relationship and refuse to leave because you're drawn to the excitement and unpredictability it provides. Perhaps you're a mom who only feels worthwhile with a schedule so overbooked you can't think straight. Perhaps you're addicted to gambling and the uncertainty, anxiety, and thrill it creates. Perhaps you're a drug- or alcohol-user who simply loves losing control over your body and mind. In all of these cases a rare god is being worshiped—the god of chaos.

To many people it's appalling. They *hate* losing control over their lives. But to a few, it feels like home.

GIFT: The Gift of Control

At this point you may think I'm sending a mixed message. I'm saying you ultimately don't have control over your life—God does. See Sarah. See Proverbs 19 v 21. At the same time, Sean's story makes it clear you're *supposed* to take control over your life. Well, which one is it?

Both...

You've Got It

God makes a bold statement about people and control in the first chapter of the Bible. At the tail end of the creation story, he says this:

> Let us make mankind in our image, in our likeness, so
> that they may rule over the fish in the sea and the birds
> in the sky, over the livestock and all the wild animals,
> and over all the creatures that move along the ground.
> (Genesis 1 v 26)

He then creates mankind, blesses them, and tells them to "fill the earth and subdue it" (v 28). God has strategically designed people to control his world—to "rule" and "subdue" it. Down to the very last slithering animal.

And if we read the rest of the Bible, it's pretty clear we're supposed to take control over *our* lives as well. Every commandment from God is him telling us to control our actions, words, thoughts, decisions, and motives in order to love him and others well. One of the fruits of the Spirit is even—you guessed it—*self-control* (Galatians 5 v 23). It's a very good thing and a gift from God.

We *should* take control over the world around us and over ourselves. It's our responsibility and our privilege as human beings created in God's image.

But He's GOT It

We just don't have *ultimate* control. Over anything. God has the final say in all things. He controls how long you live and how many kids you have. He controls when your hair turns gray and when it falls out. He controls if you get sick and if you recover. He controls how much money you make and how many promotions you get. He controls if it will be hot, cold, sunny, cloudy, windy, rainy, or snowy tomorrow. He gives life and takes it away. He's in charge of it all. We're not.

Gethsemane

So where does this leave us? How do we live in a world in which we have control but God HAS control?

I can't give you a one-size-fits-all answer, but I can direct you to a scene in the Garden of Gethsemane from the Gospel of Matthew. Jesus is about to be handed over to the Romans to be crucified. And he knows it. He's about to be tortured, whipped, flogged, beaten, mocked, stripped, and nailed to a cross. He's about to die. Worse than this, he's about to be separated from his Father. He's about to feel the deepest form of anguish possible—spiritual isolation from God.

How does he respond?

With a soul overwhelmed with sorrow to the point of death (Matthew 26 v 38), he prays. He falls facedown to the ground and says this:

> My Father, if it is possible, may this cup be taken from me. Yet not as I will, but as you will. (Matthew 26 v 39)

Jesus takes control by asking God to spare him from the suffering to come. He makes a bold appeal for mercy. But then he puts control right back where it belongs—in God's hands. He prays not for his will but for the Father's will to win out. He surrenders his life over to God, submits to his plans, and accepts the end result.

No, there's no cookie-cutter formula for when to take control and when to let go in life. But there's a posture we can *always* take—the prayerful, open-handed "not as I will, but as you will" posture of Jesus in the Garden of Gethsemane.

The true test of whether you're sipping the saltwater of control is this: can you pray the same prayer? Can you say, with confidence, "Not as I will, but as you will"?

Let me invite you to do so right now.

11. COMFORT

"I'm happy, Ahren. I'm a princess. I have everything."
"I think you're mistaking comfort for joy."

Kiera Cass, *The Heir*

11 weeks. 12 college students. 95°F (35°C). One two-bedroom apartment without air-conditioning in the most dangerous neighborhood of Chicago.

This was my summer of 2002. Twelve of us were taking part in a program known as Chicago Urban Project (CUP). The goal was to become immersed in the gang-infested Chicago neighborhood of Austin, partner with a local church, and serve the struggling community. We ran a day camp. We organized food drives. We hosted kids in the neighborhood for meals and movie nights. It was the opportunity of a lifetime.

And I hated every minute of it.

Why? It was the most uncomfortable eleven weeks of my life. I slept in a pool of sweat. I shared one bathroom with four men and seven women. I ate unhealthy low-budget meals prepared by a dozen amateur cooks. Worst of all, to teach us how to live as missionaries, CUP didn't allow us to leave the neighborhood. I couldn't walk beyond a four-block radius. I couldn't explore the city. I couldn't visit my friends, family, or girlfriend. My life wasn't my own. I was a slave to the constraints of CUP.

How did I respond? I rebelled. I broke rule after rule behind my team's back. I snuck away during free time for long runs along Lake Michigan. Every Sunday morning I drove around the city and told the team I was attending a neighborhood Catholic church (nobody was Catholic, so I was safe). I invited my girlfriend to spend a weekend with us without asking permission—an action that understandably annoyed the team. Perhaps worst of all, I was constantly bitter, antagonistic, and resentful toward my teammates. I was young, immature, and unprepared for the challenge of CUP. It showed inside and out.

In hindsight, I look at that summer as an embarrassing failure. Why? I spent it sipping saltwater—the saltwater of *comfort*. As I took sip after sip, my heart became hard, my ability to love others diminished, and my relationships with my teammates fell apart. I turned into a self-absorbed jerk. The summer was a disaster. All because I was worshiping the god of comfort.

GOD: Salvation by Ease

Comfort saltwater sippers are everywhere in today's culture. Some are spending money they don't have to buy cars, clothes, houses, handbags, trips, trinkets, machines, and massages—all to make them more comfortable. Some are sleeping in on Sunday mornings because their beds are far more comfortable than church pews. Some are avoiding difficult but necessary conversations because conflict makes them uncomfortable.

Some are dodging impactful volunteer work because it's outside their comfort zones.

It's hard to find a person who isn't sipping the saltwater of comfort. I do it all the time.

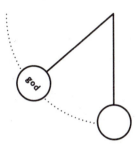

Let My People Go

In the book of Exodus, we see an entire nation of comfort saltwater sippers—the Israelites. When the book starts, they're living in Egypt. All is well for God's people for a little while, but eventually a ruthless king is put in power who tortures them and turns them into slaves. And they remain slaves for centuries.

Eventually God steps in. He wants to free the Israelites. He appears in a burning bush to a man named Moses and gives him this message:

> I have indeed seen the misery of my people in Egypt.
> I have heard them crying out because of their slave
> drivers, and I am concerned about their suffering. So I
> have come down to rescue them from the hand of the
> Egyptians and to bring them up out of that land into a
> good and spacious land, a land flowing with milk and
> honey. (Exodus 3 v 7-8)

God promises to liberate Israel from their Egyptian shackles. He sends a series of ten plagues upon the Egyptians to press them to release the Israelites. He turns the Nile—their main water source—into blood. He covers Egypt in frogs. He fills the land with gnats. He saturates all Egyptian homes with flies. He kills the country's livestock. He gives every Egyptian boils. He sends a massive hailstorm. He showers the country with plant-eating locusts. He makes the nation pitch dark for three days. He even kills all Egyptian firstborn sons.

Finally, Pharaoh—the hard-hearted Egyptian king—can't take any more. He lets God's people go.

For a second.

Almost immediately following their release, Pharaoh regrets his decision and chases the Israelites toward the Red Sea. But God counterattacks. He parts the sea, allows the Israelites to travel through, and makes the waters crash down on the Egyptians, drowning them all.

The Israelites are free! How do they respond?

By complaining.

Grinning Changes to Grumbling

Initially, the Israelites are elated by their freedom. A fresh start for the nation of Israel! Yes!

But right after crossing the Red Sea, their joy vanishes. Why? Their lives become uncomfortable. First, they're thirsty and their only water source is bitter. So they grumble to Moses. He, in turn, cries out to God. And God graciously makes their water fit to drink (Exodus 15 v 22-25).

A month and a half later, they're hungry. So they grumble again to Moses:

> If only we had died by the LORD's hand in Egypt! There
> we sat around pots of meat and ate all the food we

wanted, but you have brought us out into this desert to starve this entire assembly to death. (Exodus 16 v 3)

God again answers their grumbling with grace. He feeds them. He promises them a daily portion of manna—a flaky honey-flavored bready substance. One might think they'd be grateful for the grub. Nope. They want better-tasting food. Richer food. *Comfort* food.

So they complain again to Moses:

> If only we had meat to eat! We remember the fish we ate in Egypt at no cost—also the cucumbers, melons, leeks, onions and garlic. But now we have lost our appetite; we never see anything but this manna! (Numbers 11 v 4-6)

So God gives them meat. He covers the ground with three feet (90cm) of quail as far as a day's walk in any direction. No, this isn't a sign he's happy with the Israelites. At this point, he's infuriated by their disrespectful demand for earthly comfort. In fact, he's so angry that before they can swallow the quail, he strikes them with a massive plague (Numbers 11 v 33).

Fleeting Comfort

While this story teaches us many lessons, I'd like to focus on one: searching for lasting comfort outside of God is *pointless*.

The Israelites couldn't find lasting comfort in Egypt. They couldn't find it in the wilderness. They couldn't find it in water. Or manna. They weren't going to find it in fish, cucumbers, melons, leeks, onions, or garlic. They were never going to find lasting comfort outside of God.

And neither will we. We can move from apartments to townhomes to houses to luxury mansions, but we won't find lasting comfort in our homes. We can trade up from bicycles to used cars to new cars to new *luxury* cars, but we won't find lasting comfort in our rides. We can upgrade from three-star to four-star to five-star resorts, but we won't find lasting comfort in our vacations. We won't find it in our beds, couches, or recliners. We won't find it in our phones, tablets, or computers. We won't find it in lotions, flowers, or chocolates. *Nothing* in this world will provide comfort that lasts. Nothing.

It's all just saltwater.

GARBAGE: Salvation by Suffering

It's easy to sip the saltwater of comfort—to worship it as a god. Most of us do. But what might it look like to demonize it? To idolize *discomfort*? To glorify pain? To sip the saltwater of suffering?

A brief history lesson shows us.

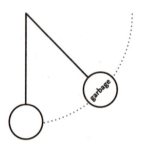

Martin Luther—the Self-Mutilating Monk

Martin Luther, famously recognized as the father of the Protestant Reformation, was also famous for gulping down the saltwater of *suffering*.

The story goes like this. In 1505, at the age of 21, Luther was traveling on horseback to college when a storm hit. After a lightning bolt struck near his feet, he freaked out. So right then and there he made a vow. He promised that if God kept him alive, he'd dedicate his life to him. He'd become a monk.

God held up his end of the deal. Two weeks later, Luther did too. He entered a monastery and began a life of religious devotion.

While at the monastery, Luther developed an obsession. He couldn't stop thinking about his sin. In particular, he couldn't stop thinking about the divine judgment awaiting him when he died. He countered his obsession with rigorous penance. He worked past exhaustion. He starved himself. He froze his body in the snow. He beat himself to unconsciousness. According to Luther, "If ever a monk got to heaven by his monkery, it was I."

But one day Luther had an epiphany. While reading the book of Romans, he realized he couldn't earn his salvation through penance or self-punishment. He couldn't earn it through *anything* he did. It could only be received by believing in Jesus, and it was *all due to God's grace.* The revelation shocked him. He couldn't do anything to make it to heaven? His church leaders had been lying to him the whole time? He'd been lying to himself?

Yep.

So on October 31, 1517, Luther nailed his 95 *Theses* to the doors of the castle church of Wittenberg, declaring, among other things, that salvation couldn't be earned—especially not by punishing oneself. It was a free gift of God given to all who believe in Christ.

The move was an act of defiance. It was the beginning of the Protestant Reformation. It was one of the most important events in the history of the church.

Some Test Questions for You

Okay, Luther's case is a dramatic one. His saltwater of suffering was exceptionally potent. But I'd argue that many of us are sipping the same drink—albeit a weaker version. How do you know if you are? Let me give you some test questions.

Do you compensate for your moral shortcomings by depriving yourself of pleasure, hoping this will somehow make you right in God's eyes? Are you uncomfortable when God blesses you with wealth or nice things? Are you proud of your suffering? Do you ever look down on others who haven't suffered as much as you?

If you've answered yes to any of these questions, you're sipping the saltwater of suffering. If so, please join me in spitting it out.

GIFT: The Gift of Comfort

My father's funeral was September 4, 2015. The service was small, quaint, and intimate—attended mostly by immediate family and my dad's close friends from work, coaching, and Alcoholics Anonymous. My sister, Michelle, read a poem. I read Scripture. Bryan gave the eulogy. I experienced a strange mix of emotions. I wept. I laughed. I felt a twinge of anger. Mostly, however, I just prayed.

After the service I had the chance to spend some time alone with my dad. For ten minutes I just stared at him and cried. There, right before me, was a man who spent his entire adult life searching for comfort. A man who foolishly thought he could find it in alcohol. A man whose life could have been so much richer, healthier, and, ironically, more comfortable had he simply given up his search for it. And now he was dead.

It was the saddest ten minutes of my life.

And then, with tears of grief pouring down my cheeks, a Scripture passage came to me:

> Praise be to the God and Father of our Lord Jesus Christ, the Father of compassion and the God of all comfort, who comforts us in all our troubles, so that we can comfort those in any trouble with the comfort we ourselves receive from God. For just as we share abundantly in the sufferings of Christ, so also our comfort abounds through Christ. (2 Corinthians 1 v 3-5)

As I meditated on these verses—right then and there over my dad's casket—my tears dried up. I wasn't sad any more. I experienced the comfort Paul describes in this passage—the comfort that my dad had been unknowingly chasing his whole life. Comfort not from this world. Comfort not in a substance, an experience, or an emotion. Comfort from Christ. Comfort *in* Christ. I didn't do anything to earn it. I *couldn't* do anything to earn it. It transformed my grief into joy. It allowed me to leave my father's funeral with a smile on my face—a smile that comes back every time I remember that day.

Pulling It All Together

No, God isn't against earthly comfort. When the Israelites cried out to him as slaves in Egypt, he *wanted* to rescue them and bring them into a "good and spacious land, a land flowing with milk and honey." And whatever your version of "milk and honey" is, he isn't opposed to you enjoying it. Enjoy your home. Enjoy your car. Enjoy your gadgets and gizmos. Enjoy the comforts of life. They're gifts from God. He isn't opposed to earthly comfort.

But if you're looking for *true* comfort, you will only find it in Jesus Christ. It isn't the same comfort you feel soaking in a warm bathtub, napping on your couch, or munching on a donut. This comfort is better. Richer. Deeper. It's a soul-permeating, heart-soothing, and lasting sense of comfort. It doesn't depend on your circumstances. It doesn't depend on your living conditions. It doesn't depend on your health, wealth, or relationships. It doesn't depend on *anything* from this world.

It depends on two things. First, it depends on what happened over 2,000 years ago. Because Christ lived a perfectly sinless life and died an infinitely uncomfortable death on the cross, we can experience comfort from above in the midst of our uncomfortable lives below.

Second, it depends on faith. You must believe in Christ and surrender your life to him. You must spit out the saltwater of comfort and drink his living water.

So take a sip. Experience *real* comfort. And share it with others. I guarantee they're looking for it too.

12. BUSYNESS

April 17th, 2011.

It was the happiest day of my life—the day I married my best friend, Abby. Our wedding was charming and unconventional. We skipped church (yes, I was a pastor, whoops!) and got married on a Sunday morning in the reception hall of a golf-course clubhouse.

My college buddy was the officiate. My 91-year-old grandpa was a groomsman. Instead of a typical reception with a DJ, bouquet toss, and awkward public garter-removal, we held a brunch service after the ceremony with 50 of our closest friends and family. It was perfect.

After the wedding came the honeymoon in Key Biscayne, a low-profile vacation spot off the coast of Miami. Abby's parents generously treated us to a five-day stay at the Ritz Carlton. This was no ordinary hotel. It was five stars of extravagant luxury—ocean views, elegant restaurants, a fancy day-spa, hot tubs carved out of natural rock, onsite tennis courts, valet car-service, a hotel staff waiting on us hand and foot... you name it. It was a chance to celebrate our new marriage in style. A chance to rest, relax, and do nothing.

And I was anxious the whole time.

Why?

I was going through saltwater withdrawal. Prior to my arrival at the Ritz, I'd been sipping the saltwater of busyness for 15 years. I'd been studying, socializing, teaching, traveling, exercising, entertaining, preaching, partying or doing *something* every waking hour of every day since I left for college. I was *always* busy. Sure, I'd taken a vacation here and there, but they were usually—and intentionally—filled with so much activity that I couldn't rest.

My withdrawal symptoms got so bad on the honeymoon that I started reading an academic paper on infant baptism at the pool just to make myself feel better. It was pitiful.

Six years later, I wish I could say I'm different. I'm not. I sip—and often gulp—the saltwater of busyness more often than I'd like to admit. In fact, guess where I'm writing the lead-in to this chapter...

Yep, on vacation. Ugh.

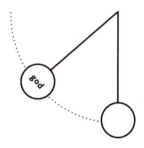

GOD: Salvation by Doing

In today's fast-paced, accomplishment-driven culture, there's always a reason to be busy. Homework needs to get done. Meals need to be cooked. Work deadlines need to be met.

Houses need to be cleaned. Books need to be written. The list is endless. There's *always* something to do. Water fountains spewing the saltwater of busyness are everywhere.

Let's look at a woman sipping the drink right in front of Jesus' face.

Martha

In the tenth chapter of the Gospel of Luke, Jesus and his traveling team of disciples make a stop in the village of Bethany. They're greeted by Martha, a hospitable woman who opens her home to Jesus. During his stay, true to character, Jesus starts to teach. Martha's sister Mary is intrigued, so she sits at his feet and listens. What does Martha do? She gets busy. The passage says she's "distracted by all the preparations that had to be made" (Luke 10 v 40). When she realizes she's the only one doing the legwork, she gets angry. Instead of rebuking her sister though, she rebukes Jesus:

> Lord, don't you care that my sister has left me to do the work by myself? Tell her to help me! (Luke 10 v 40)

His response?

> Martha, Martha ... you are worried and upset about many things, but few things are needed—or indeed only one. Mary has chosen what is better, and it will not be taken away from her. (Luke 10 v 41-42)

Jesus reprimands Martha for being busy when she needs to do one thing—rest at his feet. At the same time, he commends Mary for dropping what she's doing to focus on what's important. Not cooking. Not cleaning. Not tidying up. *Him.* He's important. He's the only thing that matters in the living room of Mary and Martha.

A Heart Issue

While there are 118 words in the story of Mary and Martha, I'd like to zero in on one. *Worried.* Jesus says that Martha was "worried" about many things as she tried to make his stay a pleasant one. Why was Martha so busy at a time when she needed to be still? Her busyness wasn't rooted in a to-do list. It was rooted in her heart. It was rooted in worry. I suspect she was worried she'd lose Jesus' approval if his accommodations weren't up to par.

Ungodly busyness, at its core, is *always* a heart issue. Both Dan and Priscilla illustrate my point:

Dan

Dan grew up in a low-income household in a rough neighborhood of suburban New Jersey. From a young age, his life goal was to get out of town and "make it." He studied day and night in high school and finished at the top of his class. He worked just as hard in college, got into a top-tier law school, and landed a job at an esteemed New York City law firm after graduation. From day one, he worked obsessively to become a partner. After 15 years of 90-hour workweeks, he achieved his goal—he's now a partner. He's "made it," right? One would think so. Not Dan. He now wants to become a *managing* partner (as high as it gets). So he's upped his work schedule to 100 hours a week. He never sees his wife or three kids. He eats three meals a day at his desk. He has no friends, no hobbies, and no fun. He's *always* busy with work. But the root of his busyness isn't his job. It's his heart. A heart driven by one thing—accomplishment. He wants to "make it."

Priscilla

Priscilla's a 25-year-old Christian woman with FOMO—Fear Of Missing Out. She's constantly afraid something epic will happen without her. So she won't say no to an invitation and her calendar is jam-packed.

Her social calendar is filled with parties, dates, coffees, happy hours, movie nights, and weekly Sunday dinners with her three best girl-friends. Her church calendar is filled with prayer meetings, singles events, Bible studies, volunteer work, and Sunday services. She's also in a running club and a book club. She's *always* busy. Not because her calendar demands it. Her *heart* demands it. It's filled with FOMO.

There's always a heart issue behind unhealthy busyness. What's yours? Perhaps you feel insecure and insignificant unless you're doing something productive. Perhaps you stay busy to distract yourself from emotional, relational, or spiritual pain in your life. Perhaps you're busy so you can brag about how busy you are. Whatever the case may be, if you're sipping the saltwater of busyness, don't check your task list. Don't check your calendar. Check your heart.

GARBAGE: Salvation by Resting

Not everybody is excessively busy. Many swing the pendulum in the opposite direction and run from being busy. They worship another god—the god of rest.

I'll give two examples.

Tyler

Tyler's a freshman at a Midwestern private university. He grew up in a high-pressure, accomplishment-driven household with domineering and demanding parents. He's living away from home for the first time. It's his first chance to take a break. His first chance to exhale. His first chance to chill out without his parents breathing down his neck.

And he's taken it to the extreme.

Tyler's committed to a life of relaxation. He sleeps until noon, spends six hours a day playing video games, and smokes a hefty amount of marijuana. He naps after both lunch and dinner. He skips most classes and does the bare minimum to keep himself off academic probation. He joined a fraternity but dropped out because of the time demands. He's stopped going to church. He's stopped working out. He's stopped doing anything productive. He spends 98% of his time in his dorm room doing one thing—relaxing.

One might shrug off Tyler's lazy lifestyle and label him a typical college freshman. I wouldn't. I'd say he's sipping saltwater—the saltwater of rest.

Joe

Joe's a 34-year-old business consultant working and living in Chicago. Kara, his wife, stays at home with their 10-month-old daughter, Chloe. Joe's job is intense and stressful. He works for a harsh boss with unreasonable expectations. His hours are long. His clients are fussy. His office is fast-paced. He works his butt off.

But wait, I thought this was the section on people worshiping the god of rest!

It is.

When Joe gets home, he checks out. Every weeknight after dinner he retreats to his basement man cave and watches TV until bedtime. He returns every Saturday morning to binge-watch Netflix dramas all day. He goes to church on Sunday mornings but rushes home to watch pro football until dinner. He won't cook. He won't clean. He won't run errands or do yard work. He's asked Kara to manage the family's finances. He does nothing for Chloe. When she wakes up crying in the middle of the night, he rolls over and lets Kara take care of her. He won't change Chloe's diapers or feed her. He'll play with her when he feels like it, but nothing more than this. He eats, sleeps, and watches TV when he's home. That's it.

To make matters worse, Joe feels completely justified in his behavior. After all, he works hard all week. He brings home the bacon. He deserves his R&R, right?

No. He's sipping saltwater. The saltwater of rest.

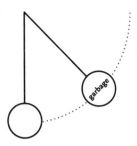

Lazy?
How do you know if you're sipping the same drink as Tyler and Joe? You're lazy. Maybe you're lazy at your job. You show up late, leave early, or take long lunches without telling anybody. Maybe you're lazy in your marriage. You've stopped showing affection toward your spouse because romance takes too much effort. Maybe you're lazy with your body. You don't exercise because vegging out is far more comfortable than working out. Maybe you're lazy in your spiritual life. You don't read the Bible because it's much easier to pick up a remote than God's word. If you're lazy with *anything*, you're sipping the saltwater of rest.

GIFT: The Gift of Busyness
Martha, Dan, Priscilla, and I have made busyness a god. We're overactive doers. Tyler and Joe treat busyness as garbage. They're lazy. How do we avoid both? What does godly busyness

look like? And furthermore, what does godly rest look like? I'll start with godly busyness.

Godly Busyness

In the 12th chapter of the Gospel of Mark, Jesus is debating with a group of religious leaders when one tries to stump him with a question:

> Of all the commandments, which is the most important?
> (Mark 12 v 28)

Jesus' response?

> "Love the Lord your God with all your heart and with all your soul and with all your mind and with all your strength." The second is this: "Love your neighbor as yourself." There is no commandment greater than these.
> (Mark 12 v 30-31)

The most important commandment is love. But what does this have to do with busyness?

In the greatest commandment, Jesus is telling us what godly busyness is. It means we're busy *loving*. Loving God and loving others.

But this love isn't about feelings. It has nothing to do with butterflies in our stomachs, sappy sentiments, or erotic impulses. Jesus is describing a different kind of love. The word translated as "love" here is the Greek word *agape*. Agape love is an act of the will independent of our emotions. It's a calculated display of benevolence toward the object of love— an intentional and unconditional demonstration of warmth, charity, honor, and respect.

How do we show God agape love? In at least three ways. First, we drink his living water. We read Scripture, spend time with other Christians, pray, show generosity, offer him praise, and tell others about him (see chapter 5, page 47). Second, we obey him (John 14 v 15). We submit to his rules, allow his word to guide us, and trust that his ways are best. Third, we love others. When we do so we're indirectly loving him: Jesus makes it clear that whatever we do to our neighbors, we do to God (Matthew 25 v 40).

How do we show agape love toward our neighbors? One word: *sacrifice*. We sacrifice our time, energy, and resources for their good. We practice patience, gentleness, and unmerited kindness even when our flesh tells us not to. We take our eyes off ourselves and focus them on those in need. We offer comfort, compassion, and care to those in pain. We're gracious toward our enemies even if they're evil back. We consider people better than ourselves and back it up with our lifestyles. We're selflessly sacrificial for the benefit of others.

What's godly busyness? We're busy loving God and loving others. We're busy obeying the greatest commandment. *That's* godly busyness.

Godly Rest

So when do we rest?

Short answer: *frequently*. It's good to rest. It's good to relax. It's good to kick up your feet after a long day of work, spend time with your family, watch a little PG-rated television, and decompress. It's good to take vacations when you're overworked, naps when you're overtired, and an occasional spa day when you're overstressed. It's good to read a book when you need peace and quiet. It's good to play sports when you need an energy outlet. It's good to do things *in moderation* that allow your mind and body to rest.

And it's *really good* to take one day a week—typically Sunday—and devote it to spiritual rest. Christians call this a "sabbath"—a day to do no work (yes, none). A day to attend church. A day to spend extra time praying, serving, worshiping, reading the Bible, and intentionally engaging with Christians. A day devoted to God.

But let me warn you. You won't find the *deepest* form of rest in anything I've listed above. You won't find it by camping out on the couch, taking a vacation, napping, soaking in a tub, reading, playing sports, or even spending a day off dedicated to God.

You'll only find it in a person.

In Matthew 11, Jesus tells us who this person is:

> Come to me, all you who are weary and burdened, and I will give you rest. Take my yoke upon you and learn from me, for I am gentle and humble in heart, and you will find rest for your souls. For my yoke is easy and my burden is light. (Matthew 11 v 28-30)

Deep, life-giving, soul-permeating rest can only be found in the person of Jesus Christ. You'll find it when you come to him and learn from him. You'll find it in his gentle spirit and humble heart. You'll find it when you let go of your burdens and release them to him. You'll find it when you accept him as your Lord, Savior, Rescuer, and Redeemer.

You'll only find *true* rest in Jesus. You'll find it when you spit out your saltwater and drink his living water.

So take a sip. And find rest for your soul.

13. PEOPLE

3 Xanax. 3 Propranolol. 3 Zoloft.

This was the prescription pill combination I took before my first sermon in New York City. Xanax—an anti-anxiety medication—calmed my nerves in a similar way to alcohol, minus the motor-skill impairment. Propranolol—a beta-blocker—slowed down my heart rate so I wouldn't get flushed or sweat profusely. Zoloft—an antidepressant—was a medication I'd been taking for ten years to keep my unpredictable emotions in check. After meeting with my psychiatrist earlier that week and sharing my fear of having a panic attack in the pulpit, she gave me the Xanax and Propranolol prescriptions in addition to my normal Zoloft refill. She said I could take one pill of each before the big sermon. 1 Xanax. 1 Propranolol. 1 Zoloft. 3 pills. That's it.

Instead I took 9.

Why? Why did I triple my dosage that day?

I was sipping saltwater. The form? People. Specifically, that morning's congregation. In the front row sat Jon Tyson—a world-class speaker, a brilliant thinker, an innovative leader, and my direct boss. The rest of the seats were filled with successful New Yorkers—high-profile investment bankers, Broadway actresses, university professors, runway models... you name it.

To me, everybody in the church that morning was impressive. And I *needed* to impress them. I needed their approval, affirmation, and acceptance. I needed them to love me. And I mean *love* me. I needed to floor them with a level of oratory excellence they'd never experienced before. And I convinced myself that the more pills I took, the likelier this would happen.

So I did something I would never recommend... something I deeply regret... something that could have killed me. I tripled my dosage. I stood up in the pulpit—high as a kite—and preached to my gods.

I may as well have been bowing down to them.

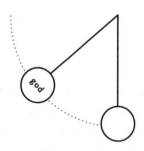

GOD: Salvation by Someone

Sipping the saltwater of people can look different for each of us. Perhaps, like me, you *need* the approval of an individual or a group and will do whatever it takes to get it. Perhaps your life loses meaning when a particular person's no longer around—maybe after a breakup or when someone dies.

Perhaps you find your identity in taking care of somebody—a sick child or an aging parent, for example. Perhaps you've allowed a love interest to replace God in your life. No matter how it may manifest itself, most of us are sipping the saltwater of people. It's a popular drink.

Let me introduce you to a set of brothers in the Bible who were gulping it down.

Jacob's Sons

In Genesis chapter 37 we're told a tragic story of sibling betrayal. Jacob—the grandson of Abraham and the son of Isaac—is the father of twelve boys. His favorite son is Joseph. To show his exceptional love for him, he makes him a fancy robe. Not surprisingly, the other brothers don't respond well:

> When his brothers saw that their father loved him more than any of them, they hated him and could not speak a kind word to him. (Genesis 37 v 4)

Joseph's brothers detest him for being daddy's favorite.

To add fuel to the fire, Joseph has a prophetic dream and shares it with his brothers:

> Listen to this dream I had: We were binding sheaves of grain out in the field when suddenly my sheaf rose and stood upright, while your sheaves gathered around mine and bowed down to it. (Genesis 37 v 6-7)

He then shares a second dream making the same point:

> I had another dream, and this time the sun and moon and eleven stars were bowing down to me. (Genesis 37 v 9)

The message of these dreams? Joseph will one day reign over his family.

Predictably, the dreams only make his brothers hate him more. So one day when they're working in a field and see Joseph approaching, they devise a plan:

> "Here comes that dreamer!" they said to each other. "Come now, let's kill him and throw him into one of these cisterns and say that a ferocious animal devoured him. Then we'll see what comes of his dreams."
> (Genesis 37 v 19-20)

Luckily for Joseph, his brother Reuben has a guilty conscience:

> When Reuben heard this, he tried to rescue him from their hands. "Let's not take his life," he said. "Don't shed any blood. Throw him into this cistern here in the wilderness, but don't lay a hand on him."
> (Genesis 37 v 21-22)

The brothers listen to Reuben's advice, take off Joseph's robe, and toss him into the cistern. But when they see a caravan of well-stocked foreign traders on their way to Egypt, their plans change. Instead of letting Joseph rot in the cistern, they sell him as a slave.

So Joseph's sent off to Egypt to spend the rest of his life as a servant. Meanwhile, the brothers slaughter a goat, dip Joseph's robe in its blood, and head home to tell Jacob that an animal's killed his favorite son, with the bloody robe as proof.

Worshiping the Wrong Father

How are Joseph's brothers drinking the saltwater of *people* in this story? Who are they worshiping? They're worshiping Jacob. More specifically, they're worshiping his love. How do we know? When they realize Jacob loves Joseph more than them, they lose their minds. They become human traffickers of *their own baby brother*. Jacob's love matters *that* much to them. With it, they're fine. Without it, they're animals.

Instead of worshiping the Father and resting in his love, they're worshiping their father and coveting his love. They're sipping the saltwater of people.

Your Human gods?
What about you? Who are you worshiping? To whom are you bonding your soul in an ungodly manner? Who are you letting direct your life? Seize your thoughts? Command your actions? Grip your soul?

Maybe it's your spouse. You're strong, confident, and secure when your marriage is solid, but you crumble at the hint of dysfunction. Maybe it's your parents. You're grown-up and married, and yet you still feel the incessant need to obey their every request. Maybe it's your therapist. You've been seeing him weekly for ten years and can't make a decision without his counsel. Maybe it's your boss, buddies, boyfriend, or best friend.

If you love anybody too much, hate anybody, or allow anybody to rule your heart, you're sipping saltwater—the saltwater of people.

GARBAGE: Salvation by Independence
Most of us are worshiping somebody. But I'd bet most of us are also worshiping "nobody." What do I mean?

On July 4th, 1776, the Declaration of Independence was approved by the United States Congress. It told the world that America was free from foreign rule. For those of us who are American, it made the core values of our country clear—life, liberty, and the pursuit of happiness.

We were autonomous. We were self-sufficient. We were on our own. Nobody could tell us what to do.

Over 240 years later, these national values have become our *personal* values. We're on our own and nobody can tell us what to do. Our money is our own. Our time is our own. Our bodies, brains, and belongings are our own. We choose how we spend our time and we choose who we spend it with. We wear what we want, eat what we want, and sleep with whoever we want. We run our lives, and if anybody has a problem with it, that's their problem. We're our own bosses. Nobody can tell us what to do.

The form of saltwater we're sipping? Call it independence. Call it freedom. Call it what you will. It has produced a nation of me-focused, individualistic, commitment-phobic lone rangers. Take Jeff as an example:

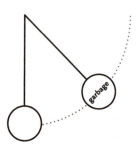

Jeff

Jeff's a 36-year-old business consultant living in center-city San Francisco. Two years ago, he met his soulmate, Deborah. They hit it off immediately and have been together ever since. They're physically attracted to each other. Their personalities fit. They connect spiritually, love each other's parents, and get along with each other's friends. All signs—and all people—

are pointing them toward marriage. Jeff knows he should pop the question. But there's one problem.

He's freaking out.

The thought of marriage terrifies him. Not because there's anything wrong with Deborah. The thought of being married to *anybody* terrifies him. His reason? Once he ties the knot, his life will no longer be his own. No more sleeping until noon. No more eating pizza five nights a week. No more leaving the toilet seat up. No more drinking milk out of the carton, leaving dirty dishes in the sink, or binge-watching sports with his buds. No more doing whatever he wants.

Plus, he'll be attached to *one person* for the rest of his life. The. Rest. Of. His. Life. He'll wake up next to Deborah every morning and eat dinner with her every evening. He'll spend every holiday with her. He'll celebrate every birthday with her. He'll attend every wedding, party, and family function with her. They'll vacation together, go to church together, and raise kids together. In Jeff's head, they'll do *everything* together. They'll be attached at the hip. And the thought of this makes him want to vomit.

Jeff knows he's at a fork in the road. He has only two options with Deborah—propose or break up. After two years, they can't just keep dating. He knows she'd be a great wife. He knows there probably isn't a better fit out there. He knows he's not getting any younger. But he also knows he can't pull the trigger. His stomach won't allow him to do so. So he's leaning toward breaking up. Correction—if he's honest with himself, he's already made the decision to break up.

Oh, and there's one detail I've left out. Since turning 30, he's been in this same position not once, not twice, but three times with three different women. And he's still single.

GIFT: The Gift of People

I worship people. So did Jacob's sons. You probably do as well. When we do, we turn them into gods. I also worship my independence. So does Jeff. You probably do as well. When we do, we turn people into garbage. Is there a healthier and holier way to live in a world of over seven billion people? How can we view people—*all* people—as gifts from God.

Would You Like to Buy a Knife?

During my second summer of college, I sold Cutco knives. I called up every adult I knew, invited myself into their homes, and gave one-hour presentations on the miracle of the Cutco knife. I'd slice through ropes, carve shapes out of leather, cut pennies in half, and belittle every other knife brand on the planet. At the end of each presentation, I'd ask them the always awkward question, "Would you like to buy this $1,200 knife set?" One person—yes, *one* person—said yes. Everybody else said no. But almost everyone bought a knife or two... I suspect out of pity for me. No, I'm certain out of pity for me.

The selling point for these ridiculously expensive knives? They never needed to be sharpened. Ever. I have no idea how this is possible. But believe me, I annoyingly repeated the line, "You'll *never* need to sharpen these knives," like a broken record. At least until they pulled out their checkbooks and bought one.

We're Not Cutco Knives

Sadly, we're not Cutco knives. We're dull, jagged, and rusted (i.e. sinful and broken). We need to be sharpened. Every single day. And God has one primary tool he uses to sharpen us—*people*. He makes this clear in the book of Proverbs:

> As iron sharpens iron, so one person sharpens another.
> (Proverbs 27 v 17)

God puts people in our lives to sharpen us. He uses people to make us holy—to craft us into those who emulate him inside and out.

He gives us spouses to expose selfishness that would otherwise go hidden in singleness. He gives us children so we'll grow in patience, perseverance, and peacemaking. He gives us bullies to show us how to love our enemies and pray for those who persecute us (Matthew 5 v 44). He gives us awful bosses so we'll learn how to submit to authority even when we want to run (Romans 13 v 1-5). He gives us abrasive and antagonistic Bible-study members to push us to love those who are difficult to love. He gives us the poor to teach us generosity, and the rich to teach us contentment. He gives us pastors to point us to God when our hearts are hard, our prayers are sparse, and our faith is weak.

God puts people—allies and enemies—in our lives to transform us into people who think and act like Jesus. To make us into people who pour out compassion, warmth, servitude, and empathy. People who love not only those who love us, but those who hate us as well. People who mirror the only person who—like a Cutco knife—never needed to be sharpened.

They're All Gifts

My encouragement to you is this: view every person in your life as a gift. View the good ones—those who make you laugh, support you in your suffering, and fill you with joy—as gifts. But also view the bad ones—those who make you cry, abandon you in your suffering, and cause you anxiety—as gifts.

Why? Because both sets of people have been hand-planted by the fingers of God to change you. To make you better. To make you holier.

To mold you into a Jesus look-alike.

14. FOOD

Jane Fonda, Lady Gaga, Katie Couric, Fiona Apple, Elton John, Lindsay Lohan, Audrey Hepburn, Janet Jackson, Meredith Vieira, Richard Simmons, Alanis Morissette, Joan Rivers, Paula Abdul, Princess Diana, Kelly Clarkson, Russell Brand, Sharon Osbourne, Wynonna Judd, Sally Field, and Oprah Winfrey.

What do these 20 celebrities have in common? All of them have struggled with eating disorders. And they've been brave enough to go public with their struggles.

So I guess I should too.

My unhealthy relationship with food was brief, lasting just six months in my late 20s while I was pastoring in Manhattan. I wasn't technically anorexic. Or bulimic. I'm not sure clinicians would even label my actions a real eating disorder. But I would.

It all started with a 40-day fast. During this particular fast, I chose not to eat from sunrise to sunset. Since I never woke up before dawn, this meant skipping breakfast, lunch, and any snacks. Once the sun went down, I was free to eat whatever I wanted. And boy did I. Come dusk, I would *gorge* myself. I'd eat a 2,000-calorie dinner, top it off with two or three desserts, and keep snacking until my head hit the pillow. I never really stopped eating from sunset to bedtime.

And I considered this a "fast."

After the 40 days were up, I was free to resume my normal breakfast-lunch-snack-dinner routine. But I didn't. Why not? I'd fallen in love with the starve-gorge-rinse-repeat rhythm. It allowed me to eat like a king—at least at night—and not gain weight since I was depriving myself during the day. I could enjoy food as I never had before and remain trim. I loved it.

But what was *really* going on during those six months? I was swinging the food pendulum from one extreme to the other every night and day. At night I was idolizing food—treating it as a god. During the day I was demonizing food—treating it as garbage. Back and forth the pendulum swung for half a year. I was completely mistreating a good and gracious gift from God.

You might be too.

GOD: Salvation by Eating

Sipping the saltwater of food—idolizing it—doesn't necessarily mean being gluttonous like me. It might not even involve overeating. Any time we allow food to control us—to steer us away from God—we turn it into a god.

Just like Esau...

Esau

In Genesis 25, we're introduced to Esau, the twin brother of Jacob, son of Isaac, and grandson of Abraham. One day, Jacob and Esau are doing what they do best—Jacob's home cooking stew and Esau's out hunting. When Esau returns, he's famished. He begs Jacob for some stew. Jacob's response?

First, sell me your birthright. (Genesis 25 v 31)

Esau's reply?

Look, I am about to die ... What good is the birthright to me? (Genesis 25 v 32)

So Esau swears an oath to Jacob and sells him his birthright. Jacob gives him the grub, and Esau takes off with a full belly. And no birthright.

Esau gives up his birthright for a bowl of stew. A. Bowl. Of. Stew. To understand how ludicrous this is, we need to understand a bit about Esau's birthright. In ancient Near-Eastern culture, being the firstborn male was significant. Esau has special status as Isaac's oldest son. He's the principle heir to his family's fortunes—likely in line to receive double Jacob's inheritance (Deuteronomy 21 v 17). Plus, his family's *loaded*. Genesis 13 v 2 says Abraham "had become very wealthy in livestock and in silver and gold." This wealth has already been passed down to Isaac, and soon it will be passed down to Jacob and Esau, with Esau getting most of it. So Esau's giving up a ton of money and possessions by selling his birthright to Jacob.

But Esau's birthright is especially valuable for another reason. There's a *spiritual* component to it. Back in Genesis 12, God said this to Abraham:

I will make you into a great nation, and I will bless you;
I will make your name great, and you will be a blessing.
I will bless those who bless you, and whoever curses
you I will curse; and all peoples on earth will be blessed
through you. (Genesis 12 v 2-3)

At the end of this passage, "through you" also means "through your family line." This means Esau is the natural heir to receive this same set of blessings from God. He'll be the head of a great nation with God guiding it. He'll have a great name. He'll bless others. In fact, the *entire world* will be blessed through him.

This is Esau's birthright.

But Esau doesn't care. He's hungry. He turns it all down for a lousy bowl of stew. In doing so, he's slapping God in the face. In this moment, his empty stomach is his greatest priority. Food is controlling him. It's his god.

I'll admit Esau's story is a unique one. Birthrights are a thing of the past and stew is a rare form of currency today. But that doesn't make Esau's story irrelevant. He sipped the saltwater of food and gave up blessings as a result. And if we sip the same drink, we'll give up blessings as well. Take Doug as an example:

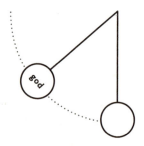

Doug

Doug's a 37-year-old computer programmer who works from home. He's a Christian and attends church every Sunday, but he's struggled to make friends for years. He spends most of his time isolated in his studio apartment and is quite lonely. To cope with his loneliness, he does one thing. *He eats*. It isn't uncommon for him to consume 7,000 calories in a day. Not surprisingly, he's obese. He's ashamed of his appearance, which causes him to isolate himself even more. He eats because he's lonely. He's lonely because he eats. It's a vicious cycle.

What blessings has Doug given up by sipping the saltwater of food? What is *his* version of Esau's birthright? He's given up a clear conscience. He feels guilty every morning, knowing he overate the day before. He's given up his health. He's slowly destroying his body with every gluttonous meal. He's given up freedom. He's clearly addicted to food—smack-dab in the middle of the saltwater cycle. He's given up money. Half his monthly paycheck goes toward food. Ultimately, he's given up holiness. He's living in sin—sipping the saltwater of food daily—and he knows God isn't okay with it.

Doug has a choice. He can cope with his loneliness by eating, or he can turn to Christ for companionship. He can treat food as his friend, or he can see Christ as a friend (John 15 v 15) and work extra hard to make friends at church. He can continue sipping the saltwater of food, or he can spit it out.

And if you're sipping the same drink, so can you.

GARBAGE: Salvation by Starving

It's quite common to idolize food—to treat it as a god. But it's also common to demonize food—to treat it as garbage. And when we do so, we're usually worshiping another set of gods.

Take Anna as an example...

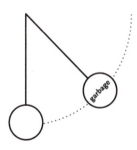

Anna

Anna's a 17-year-old only child in a rich suburb of Washington, D.C. Her parents have an awful relationship. Her dad, Ron, is a heavy drinker and an angry drunk. He does three things every night—down scotch, scream at his wife, and pass out. Anna's mom, Tara, is no pushover, so she screams back—repeatedly demeaning her husband with profanity-laced insults. They slam doors, punch walls, and regularly throw lamps, vases, and plates. They hate each other and they've created a home of chaos for their daughter.

To make matters worse, Tara is a hypercritical mom. She's particularly prone to criticize Anna's weight. She routinely asks about her diet and comments on her appearance. When Anna looks thin, Tara compliments her. When Anna doesn't—at least in Tara's eyes—she lets her know. Her love for Anna is directly tied to her weight.

Throughout her teenage years, Anna has tried to do two things—gain control over her chaotic life and please her domineering mother. She's found a way to kill two birds with one stone. She starves herself. Over the last four years, her daily calorie-intake has plummeted from 2,000 to 200. She can feel her ribs through her shirt. She wears child-sized tops. She looks like a skeleton with skin.

Even though Anna's friends have confronted her about her diet and appearance, she has no desire to change. After all, why would she? In her mind, her eating disorder only benefits her. It gives her control. It pleases her mom. Why give this up just for a little food?

What has Anna done? In worshiping control and human approval, she's demonized food. It's become her enemy. She sees it as a necessary evil to survive, but that's it. To Anna, food is garbage. Which is where it usually ends up anyway.*

GIFT: The Gift of Food

Many of us are either idolizing or demonizing food. So how *should* we view it appropriately?

Beyond Sustenance

Let's face it—without food, we're dead. It's fuel for our bodies. It's God's gift to sustain us. But is that it? Is food only meant for sustenance?

No way. The Bible shows us that God's gift of food transcends mere sustenance. For example, in the Old Testament, the nation of Israel uses it to celebrate. They show gratitude for God's provision and redeeming power with three annual feasts (Exodus 23 v 14-17). Food's also critical to the Old Testament sacrificial system. Grains and meats are burned on the altar as a way to worship God and atone for sin (Leviticus 1 – 16). God even uses food to train the Israelites. In the wilderness, he provides manna daily—and only daily—to condition them to depend on *him*—not on themselves—for their survival (Exodus 16).

In the New Testament, Jesus uses food to perform miracles— feeding 5,000 with five loaves of bread and two fish, for example (John 6 v 1-13). At the Last Supper, he uses bread and wine to explain his upcoming death to his disciples (Mark 14 v 12-26). In the future, he'll use food to celebrate God's final victory over

Satan and death at a lavish wedding feast with him and his bride, the church (Revelation 19 v 6-9). Yes, food is used for far more than sustenance throughout the Bible.

And God has given *us* food for much more than sustenance. He's given it for pleasure. He's intentionally designed us so that our tastebuds interact with food's flavor to create feelings of happiness. He's given it to unite us with others. We celebrate holidays, meet potential business-partners, and have first dates over meals. God has even given it as a way to show love. When we cook for others, take friends out to dinner, and provide meals for those in need, we're loving them and loving God in the process.

Food is meant for far more than sustenance. It's a blessing from God—his delicious gift to us.

Four Test Questions

So how do you know if you're neither idolizing nor demonizing food? How do you know if you're approaching it as a gift from above—nothing more and nothing less? Let's get super practical for a moment and ask four test questions:

First, are you praying before you eat? *Earnestly* praying and thanking God for the food you're about to eat? It's easy to forget that food is a gift from God—a blessing straight from his hand—if you're not actively recognizing it as such through prayer. So say grace. Not as a legalistic ritual, but as a heartfelt expression of gratitude to the One who has provided your food.

Second, are you eating an appropriate amount of food each day (with wiggle room, of course)? Not too much. Not too little. I'm not a dietician, and each person's body and metabolism are unique, so I can't give an exact formula for the right number of calories you should be consuming. And exceptions can certainly be made—holidays and celebrations, for example. But in general, is your daily food intake neither too high nor too low?

Third, are you eating in a healthy rhythm? Perhaps a breakfast-lunch-snack-dinner rhythm works for you. Or perhaps you prefer to eat five or six smaller meals a day to space things out. The point is you're not copying me in Manhattan—eating once a day—or Doug—eating *all* day—or Anna—*never* eating.

Fourth, are you enjoying your food? Our taste buds are all different so there's no uniform amount of pleasure we're supposed to experience when eating. But are you at least recognizing that food is *supposed* to be pleasurable? That God has designed it as a source of delight? That it's not something to—literally speaking—spit out?

Ask yourself these four test questions. They're a good starting place to see if you're handling food rightly—as a gift from God.

Real Food

But if we're going to understand the *real* gift of food, we have to look beyond what goes into our stomachs. The real gift of food can't be found in a grocery store, restaurant, or farmers' market. It isn't even edible. In John 6, Jesus tells us what the real gift of food is.

It's himself.

Huh?

Just after feeding the 5,000, Jesus is teaching before a large Jewish crowd in a synagogue in Capernaum on the north shore of the Sea of Galilee. He says this:

> Very truly I tell you, unless you eat the flesh of the Son
> of Man and drink his blood, you have no life in you.
> Whoever eats my flesh and drinks my blood has eternal

life, and I will raise them up at the last day. For my flesh
is real food and my blood is real drink. (John 6 v 53-55)

What's Jesus talking about? Is he calling them to cannibalism, with himself as their first meal? No. To eat his flesh and drink his blood is code for believing in Jesus and devoting our lives to him. What does he promise if we do so? He promises more than food could ever provide. He promises lasting satisfaction (John 6 v 35). He promises unconditional acceptance (v 37). He promises eternal life (v 40). He promises we'll be firmly united with him now and forever (v 56).

Jesus symbolically refers to himself as food. But he's infinitely better than food. He's God. And only he can feed your *soul*. So join me in spitting out the saltwater of food and feasting on a different meal. A meal that has nothing to do with eating. A meal more delicious than anything this world could cook up.

I promise, you'll never be hungry again.

---

* *A quick disclaimer. I understand that my description of Anna's eating disorder may sound simplistic. I recognize that anorexia is a confusing, complex, and catastrophic clinical problem affecting the mind, body, and soul. It has many roots. In Anna's case, the root is idolatry, but I'm not suggesting this must always be the case. If anorexia (or any eating disorder) is something that you (or someone you know) are struggling with, please talk to a counselor, pastor, or trusted Christian friend about it.*

15. WORKS

"25 Our Fathers and 25 Hail Marys, please. Oh... and on your knees."

This was my assignment from a Catholic priest after I'd formally confessed my sins to him one afternoon in the spring of 1999. I was in a season of spiritual curiosity and, having grown up Catholic, decided to re-explore my childhood faith. I thought the confession booth was a good place to start. After sharing my synopsis of a decade of sins in about 15 minutes, the priest thanked me for my honesty and told me I'd be forgiven by God if I prayed the 50 prayers. So I went straight to the sanctuary, pulled down the kneeler, and cranked 'em out.

How'd I feel afterwards? Exhilarated. I'd erased a decade of debauchery with one confession session and a quick spiritual homework assignment. Ten years of rebellion swept away in a half hour. I was pardoned, purified, and protected from God's wrath. My conscience was clear. God loved me again. It felt amazing.

How'd I respond?

I called up my buds, went straight to the bars, and got drunk.

My justification in doing so? I could go back to the same confession booth the next week, jump through the same set of hoops, and be forgiven again. I'd share the evening's shenanigans with the priest and do another set of his religious exercises—and he'd wipe my slate clean. I'd be back on a pathway to heaven.

Instead, I was on a pathway to hell.

GOD: Salvation by Piety

Why? Why was I so wrong about my spiritual trajectory that day? I was sipping saltwater. The form? Works. What's a work? Any well-intentioned word, deed, or discipline. It can be God-focused—a religious ritual, spiritual regimen, or expression of holy devotion. It can be people-focused—a loving letter, gracious gift, warmhearted word, or encouraging e-mail. It can be any positively motivated action directed upward or outward.

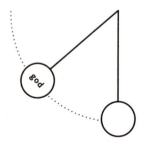

While few Christians would say we can be saved by works, many of us live as if we can be. When we pray, fast, serve, tithe, and evangelize, we think God loves us more. When we lie, cheat, steal, fight, envy, boast, covet, or cuss, we think God loves us less. We live as if our standing before God depends on our performance. We sip the saltwater of works.

Just like the Pharisee from the 18th chapter of the Gospel of Luke...

The Pharisee and the Tax Collector

In Luke 18, Jesus tells a parable about two men. One's a Pharisee—a member of a rigid Jewish sect known for their strict obedience to God's laws (and a few of their own). The other's a tax collector—a member of a profession known for greed, deception, and corrupt business practices. The story goes like this:

> Two men went up to the temple to pray, one a Pharisee and the other a tax collector. The Pharisee stood by himself and prayed: "God, I thank you that I am not like other people—robbers, evildoers, adulterers—or even like this tax collector. I fast twice a week and give a tenth of all I get."
>
> But the tax collector stood at a distance. He would not even look up to heaven, but beat his breast and said, "God, have mercy on me, a sinner." (Luke 18 v 10-13)

Jesus then states the fate of the two.

> I tell you that this man [the tax collector], rather than the other [the Pharisee], went home justified before God. For all those who exalt themselves will be humbled, and those who humble themselves will be exalted. (v 14)

Jesus vindicates the tax collector and condemns the Pharisee. Why?

We'll start with the tax collector. Jesus says he'll be exalted. For what reason? He's humble before God (v 14). His position, posture, and penitent pounding of his chest reveal a heart that knows it's sinful.

The tax collector knows he's been drunk on saltwater for quite a while—albeit in a different form than the Pharisee—and that he deserves punishment. He knows he has only one chance for salvation, and it isn't his works. It's God's mercy. As a result, Jesus declares him righteous.

At the same time, Jesus condemns the Pharisee. Why? He doesn't condemn him for his obedience to God's commands. God wouldn't give commands if he didn't desire obedience to them. He doesn't condemn him for avoiding evil. God abhors evil and wants us to run from it. Jesus condemns the Pharisee because he's standing on a self-made spiritual pedestal. He believes he's earned God's stamp of approval by obeying the Torah to a T. And he's proud of it. He's looking down on everybody else for their lack of holiness (Luke 18 v 9). He's arrogantly sipping the saltwater of works. And Jesus reveals his fate. He'll be humbled.

What's the Big Deal?

Why does God hate it so much when we sip the saltwater of works? Three reasons.

First, it's blasphemy. When we drink it, we're saying we have the power to pay the penalty for our sins. We're saying we—mere mortals created by the infinitely holy God—can appease his wrath. That we have the ability to bridge the sin-caused chasm between us and God. That we can do what only God can do—reconcile ourselves to himself. That we are saviors—not him. It's blasphemy.

Second, when we sip the saltwater of works, we become self-righteous. In Ephesians 2, the apostle Paul says this:

> For it is by grace you have been saved, through faith—
> and this is not from yourselves, it is the gift of God—not
> by works, **so that no one can boast**.
> (Ephesians 2 v 8-9, bold text mine)

Paul knows we'll boast if we think our works have saved us. We'll become puffed up just like the Pharisee. We'll become proud of our piety. And the book of Proverbs makes it clear how God feels about the proud:

> The LORD detests all the proud of heart. Be sure of this:
> They will not go unpunished. (Proverbs 16 v 5)

Third, when we sip the saltwater of works, it makes the cross pointless. If we can save ourselves through our spiritual performance, that means God didn't have to kill his Son. Jesus didn't have to be mocked, whipped, flogged, or beaten. Nails didn't have to be pounded through his wrists. He didn't have to experience infinite separation from the Father. The crucifixion was unnecessary—a futile miscue on God's part. When we sip the saltwater of works, we're saying that Jesus' greatest act of love—laying down his life for us (1 John 3 v 16)—wasn't love. It was stupid.

God *hates* it when we sip the saltwater of works. It's blasphemous, it breeds self-righteousness, and it erodes the power of the cross. If you're drinking it, please—I beg you—join me in spitting it out.

GARBAGE: Salvation by License

Many of us are sipping the saltwater of works. We believe they can save us and we treat them as gods. Are there people who swing the pendulum in the opposite direction? Who treat works as garbage? There are. And some profess to be Christians. Just like Will:

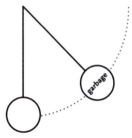

Will

Will's a college student at a state university in rural Texas. He attended a 20,000-member suburban megachurch growing up. The message of the church was the same every Sunday: God loves you! He. Loves. You. He loves you so much—so much—that he was willing to send his Son to die for your sins. There's *nothing* you can do to earn your salvation. There's *nothing* you can do to lose it as long as you believe in him. It's all about grace. Grace. Grace. Grace.

While this message of grace is technically true, the pastors of the church strategically left out other parts of the Bible. Specifically, the parts about God's holiness and his demand for *our* holiness (for example, 1 Peter 1 v 15-16). The pastors never spoke about God's rigid moral code. They never mentioned our need to repent when we break it. They never talked about God's desire for us to do good works. They never taught that genuine faith should *always* result in good works.

They focused all their attention on Ephesians 2:

> For it is by grace you have been saved, through faith—
> and this is not from yourselves, it is the gift of God—not
> by works, so that no one can boast. (Ephesians 2 v 8-9)

But left out James 2:

> As the body without the spirit is dead, so faith without
> deeds [i.e. works] is dead. (James 2 v 26)

Since Will's pastors never talked about God's demand for holiness and good works, he thinks it's fine to live however he wants—as long as he believes in Jesus. So he's knee-deep in a life of sin. He's sleeping around. He's addicted to pornography. He gets drunk daily. He copies his friends' homework assignments and cheats in his exams. He's rude, crude, and crass. He feels no conviction. No guilt. No sorrow, remorse, or impulse to change. And to make matters worse, he's abandoned every spiritual discipline his parents taught him growing up. He skips church. He keeps his Bible shut. He doesn't pray. The only person he serves is himself. Nobody on campus knows he's a Christian. But he's certain he's going to heaven. He's convinced he's saved because of his faith in Christ.

The problem? He's not. His faith is without works. So it's dead.

Insurance Policy?

Does Will's story connect with you? Even a little bit? Are there times when you turn God's grace into a license to sin? Do you believe God is so loving and merciful that he'll wave you into heaven no matter how you live? Is Christ a mere insurance policy to protect you from damnation after death? Do you, like Will, see spiritual disciplines as futile? Do you consider works ultimately unnecessary?

Put bluntly, would you call yourself a Christian and yet you live like everybody else? If so—like Will—your faith is dead. And your eternal destiny is in danger.

GIFT: The Gift of Works

Some of us live like the Pharisee. We treat works as gods. Some of us live like Will. We treat works as garbage. Both approaches are wrong. How, then, should we view works?

Motivation Is Everything

First, motivation is *everything* when it comes to works. We can do exceptional works for the wrong reasons, and God sees them as filthy rags (Isaiah 64 v 6). What should a Christian's motivation be for doing good works? We shouldn't do them to be saved; we should do them because we're *already* saved. We shouldn't obey God to earn his favor; we should obey him because we *already* have it. We shouldn't pray, serve, fast, attend church, or read the Bible to rescue ourselves from hell; we should do these things because we've *already* been rescued from hell. We're saved by grace through faith in Christ, and our salvation should result in good works.

Put another way, if we do good works to earn salvation, they're motivated by selfishness. They're manipulative tactics to gain spots in heaven. And they're an abomination to God. If, instead, our works are motivated by gratitude for *already* having salvation, they honor God. They're worshipful responses to a salvation that's secure. And he loves them.

Motivation is everything when it comes to works.

Blessing Is Our Reward

Second, God will reward us for doing good works. His reward? We'll be "blessed." The writer of the very first psalm says this:

> Blessed is the one who does not walk in step with the wicked or stand in the way that sinners take or sit in the company of mockers, but whose delight is in the law of the LORD, and who meditates on his law day and night.
> (Psalm 1 v 1-2)

The psalm writer is describing a person avoiding evil. A person committed to holiness. A person obsessed with the law of the Lord—the Bible. A person who delights in it, meditates on it constantly, and obeys it. He's describing a person doing good works. He says this person will be "blessed."

How does God bless us when we do good works? He doesn't necessarily make us happy. Or healthy. Or handsome, hip, or hitched. Instead, as we do good works, he changes us. Verse 3 tells us how:

> That person is like a tree planted by streams of water, which yields its fruit in season, and whose leaf does not wither—whatever they do prospers. (Psalm 1 v 3)

As we do good works, God molds us into fruit-producers. We become more loving. More patient. More kind, loyal, gentle, and self-controlled. Our words become more uplifting. Our actions become more selfless. Even when the heat rises and the rain stops—when temptations arise—we continue to produce fruit. We become who we were meant to be before the fall. We become more of who we'll be in paradise.

As we do good works, we become more like Jesus. *That's* how God blesses us.

The Greatest Blessing

But the greatest blessing we receive because of works has nothing to do with *our* works. We're blessed because of another person's works. A set of works that were infinitely holier and more sacrificial than anything you or I could do.

I'm talking about the works of Christ. What did he do? First, he obeyed the Father perfectly. He never worshiped an idol. He never took the Lord's name in vain. He always kept the Sabbath and honored his parents. He never murdered, committed adultery, stole, lied, or coveted. He never felt an ounce of unholy anger. He was never lazy or lustful. He was never greedy or gluttonous. He never sipped a drop of saltwater. He was tempted in every way as we are and yet never sinned (Hebrews 4 v 15). He loved the Father perfectly by obeying him perfectly.

Second, Jesus loved others perfectly. He put their needs above his. He fed the hungry. He ate with outcasts. He washed his disciples' feet. He prayed for both his friends and enemies. He was gentle when the situation called for gentleness, and stern when it called for sternness. He showed unmatched kindness. He was unwaveringly patient. He was unconditionally caring, considerate, and compassionate. He was love in human form. Every day of his life.

But Jesus' greatest work—his greatest act of love—didn't take place until the day he died. It took place on the cross. There, he died a death he never should have died. A death he intentionally chose to die. A death reserved only for sinners like you and me. A death as painful as hell itself. A death he died out of love. Love for the Father. Love for others. Indescribable love. *Perfect* love.

Why are these works—*Christ's* works—his perfect life and sacrificial death—such a blessing to us? Because they've secured our salvation. They are enough to appease the wrath of God (Romans 5 v 9). They've opened the door for us to have a relationship with the Father now and forever. Because of the life and death of Jesus Christ, we've been given paradise. Tastes of paradise now. Eternal paradise to come.

But there are two conditions for this to be true for *you*. First, you must place your faith in him. You must believe that Jesus' spotless life and selfless death were necessary and sufficient to save you. Second, you must stop trying to save *yourself*. You must spit out the saltwater of works. You must stop trying to earn a spot in heaven by sinning less, obeying more, and "being a good person." You must rest in the fact that Jesus was the perfect person and *that* is enough.

Will you?

A BRIEF NOTE ABOUT DAD

To Dad. I'll see you soon.

As this book comes to an end, you might be wondering why I chose this as my opening dedication. I didn't choose it because my dad quit drinking and we became best friends. He didn't quit drinking. We didn't become best friends. So why did I choose it?

I'll start with the *"To Dad"* portion. I chose this as an expression of forgiveness. Dad, I forgive you. I forgive you for abandoning our family when we needed you. I forgive you for lying to us and pretending to be someone you weren't. I forgive you for allowing alcohol to sever our father-son relationship. I forgive you for not attending my wedding. I forgive you for hurting Mom. I forgive you for sipping saltwater. Why? Because Christ has forgiven me. Out of the forgiveness I've received, I forgive you.

Next, the second part—*"I'll see you soon."* Why did I write this? For one reason. On a Saturday afternoon three weeks before my father died, I came over to his house. I caught him on a day when he was exceptionally coherent and talkative. I admittedly went there with an agenda—I was going to read the Bible to him. Specifically, the Gospel of John. A half hour into my visit, he became tired and needed to lay his head down to rest. I knew this was my chance. So I asked if I could read to him while he relaxed. He said yes.

For the next 45 minutes, I read Scripture to my father. After each chapter, I asked him if he wanted me to stop. It wasn't until I finished John 6 that he said yes. I then asked him a question.

"Dad?"

"Yeah?"

"Everything that I just read... do you believe it?"

He paused.

"I do."

"No really, Dad, *do you believe it*?" I needed to make sure he understood the weight of my question and his response. "Do you believe in Jesus? Do you believe that you're a sinner in need of grace? Do you believe that Jesus lived, died, and was resurrected from the dead to save you? Do you believe that trusting in Christ right now means you are forgiven forever? For everything? For *everything*? Are you willing to surrender your life to him?"

He paused again.

"Yes."

And at that point, I believe my father became a Christian. He drank living water for the first time. Ten minutes after hearing the story of Insatia at the well.

My dad died on August 27th, 2015. He didn't have much time after our conversation to live out his faith. But, as with the thief on the cross (Luke 23 v 40-43), it didn't matter. He gave his life to Christ. He let go. He offered his soul to God. And I believe he's in paradise.

Dad, I'll see you soon.

THANK YOU...

Thanks to all who have made *Sipping Saltwater* a joy to write. Thanks to Abby for encouraging me every step of the way. Thanks to Alison for gently and patiently teaching me how to write with clarity and biblical accuracy. Thanks to Tim, Jon, and Ed for their invaluable mentorship at different points in my pastoral career. This book would not be possible without you all.

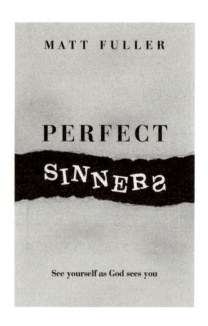

The Bible tells Christians that we are loved by God, no matter what we've done, but that we are also sinners called to put to death the sin in our lives. Holding both truths together in balance can be tricky, but it's essential for healthy Christian living. Overemphasising one at the expense of the other causes all sorts of problems.

Perfect Sinners will help us keep the balance, as we distinguish between our "status" before God and our "walk" with him.

JOHN HINDLEY

DEALING
with
DIS
A
P
P
O
I
N
T
M
E
N
T
...

*How to know joy when life
doesn't feel great*

Life is disappointing. And disappointment can so easily come to dominate our life—the nagging thought in the back of our minds and the constant "but" coloring all our pleasures.

In this realistic, hope-filled book, John Hindley shows how to deal with disappointment—what disappointment is, what it does, and how to learn to live with the disappointments while also knowing joy.

thegoodbook.co.uk thegoodbook.com

the good book

COMPANY

BIBLICAL | RELEVANT | ACCESSIBLE

At The Good Book Company, we are dedicated to helping Christians and local churches grow. We believe that God's growth process always starts with hearing clearly what he has said to us through his timeless word—the Bible.

Ever since we opened our doors in 1991, we have been striving to produce resources that honor God in the way the Bible is used. We have grown to become an international provider of user-friendly resources to the Christian community, with believers of all backgrounds and denominations using our Bible studies, books, evangelistic resources, DVD-based courses and training events.

We want to equip ordinary Christians to live for Christ day by day, and churches to grow in their knowledge of God, their love for one another, and the effectiveness of their outreach.

Call us for a discussion of your needs or visit one of our local websites for more information on the resources and services we provide.

Your friends at The Good Book Company

NORTH AMERICA thegoodbook.com 866 244 2165
UK & EUROPE thegoodbook.co.uk 0333 123 0880
AUSTRALIA thegoodbook.com.au (02) 9564 3555
NEW ZEALAND thegoodbook.co.nz (+64) 3 343 2463

 WWW.CHRISTIANITYEXPLORED.ORG
Our partner site is a great place for those exploring the Christian faith, with a clear explanation of the good news, powerful testimonies and answers to difficult questions.